"Singing the Tear. MW01598912 e transition of four immigrant families to America, and their experiences in their new homes. Gustaff uses family lore backed up with solid documentation, local history, and a dose of imagination to put meat on the bare bones of a family history. The result is a fascinating journey from Lithuania and Poland to the coal regions of Pennsylvania. The reader learns not just how and where these families came to settle in America, but gets to see their dreams and fears unfold in vignettes of family life. In these pages we can catch glimpses of our own ancestors. The mix of sorrow and anticipation when leaving the old world, never again to see family and friends. The heartswell of marriages and births, and the despair of sickness and funerals against the steady drumbeat of jobs and daily domestic life. This book will be of interest not just to those who descend from these particular immigrant families, but to anyone whose families left their homes to follow the vision of a better life. It will be especially interesting to anyone whose families lived in the American northeast during the turn of the twentieth century."

David Neimeyer, professional genealogist, college professor, and retired Naval Officer, a specialist on Pennsylvania immigrant genealogy.

"I have read many 'Roots'-oriented family histories - the search for one's own ancestry - and have always yearned to read one tracing a Lithuanian family. *Singing the Tears* combines family history, memorable events that are familiar to all Lithuanians, and personal aspects that tug at heart strings to bring forth a book that truly represents many Lithuanians' experiences. Leona Gustaff brings the reader into her family's living room with her easy storytelling style and wonderful family recipes."

Rasa Ardys-Juska, editor of Bridges, an English-language monthly for Americans of Lithuanian heritage.

"All too often genealogists are content to provide the basic facts about their ancestry. These publications do serve a useful purpose, but often to a limited number of direct descendants. Leona Gustaff has shown in this work that a genealogy can serve a wider purpose and provide a resource which appeals to a wider audience than those fortunate enough to be related to the families chronicled.

"Mrs. Gustaff's work is a social history which places her family in a historical context that posits them as historical actors, not merely passive people overwhelmed by circumstance. I can certainly attest to her careful research, having had the pleasure of working with her while she was undertaking research at the Special Collections Department, Langsdale Library, University of Baltimore."

Thomas L. Hollowak, head of archives and special collections at the University of Baltimore and an internationally recognized authority on the Polish-American immigration.

"Leona Gustaff has done something wonderful. In telling the stories of her family, she has bequeathed to them a treasure trove of tales. More importantly, for the rest of us, Mrs. Gustaff reminds us once more of the immigrant experience. And, in this particular case, we have these stories of Lithuanian immigrants which helps fill a void in our understanding of their assimilation into American life."

John Kenneth White, Professor of Politics at the Catholic University of America.

SINGING THE TEARS

SINGING THE TEARS
THE IMMIGRANT JOURNEY

LEONA SHIERANT GUSTAFF

09 08 07 06 05 04 03   5 4 3 2 1

ISBN 0-9728499-0-4

Contents

Preface

To my knowledge, no family history exists for the Guzevicius/ Gustaff, Kubilius, Matusevicius, or Sierant/Shierant families from which my husband and I are descended.* This book is meant to help fill that gap. My intention in writing it has been to leave our children a legacy, a family heritage, that I hope will be treasured and shared with their offspring and with generations yet to come. At the same time I hope that the "immigrant journeys" recounted here may be of interest to a wider audience, offering insight into times, places, and experiences that are already rapidly fading from living memory.

This is the story of my grandparents, my parents, and my husband's parents, all of whom were immigrants (in one case the son of immigrants) who came to America in the great migration from Eastern Europe around the turn of the last century. This book is the story of that migration as lived by real people—people leaving their homelands never to return, making a life in a new world, facing challenges with courage, and launching their children into lives of opportunity and fulfillment while also preserving old-country traditions that continue to give those lives a rich and piquant flavor.

In addition to the immigrant experience, all of these people shared the experience of life in America in the twentieth century—an extraordinary time that future generations may find stranger than fiction. The people in this book lived through World War I, World War II, and the Great Depression. In their lifetime they saw many dramatic changes in everyday life—changes from the coal stove to the gas stove, gas light to electric light, horse and buggy

---

*For help in understanding the complexities of Lithuanian family names, and in keeping track of the various names and nicknames used in referring to the same individual at different places in this book, please see the "Note on Names," pp. xxvii -xxx, especially Table 1, "Dramatis Personae."

For help in pronouncing names and other words from non-English languages, see Table 2, "Pronunciation Guide," also in the "Note on Names."

to automobile, washing clothes by hand to the washing machine, ice box to refrigerator, and many more.

Having lived together with most of them (I never knew my father's parents), I tried to write the words they would speak and tell you about their lives as they immigrated to America.

I have felt the pain of my grandparents, Jan, Ana, Martinas, and Ona, and my husband's parents, Juozas and Ona, as they departed from their families in the old country knowing that they would probably never meet again. I recognized the thrill of their hope and excitement as they looked forward to a promising life in a new and strange land.

I was amazed to discover how they suffered with tact and discipline the difficulties they encountered in the new world. They accepted danger, hard work, strange customs, new friends, challenges, and opportunities as they struggled to make better lives for themselves and their children.

I enjoyed immensely writing the stories of lives of past family members and the times and places in which they lived. It took me nearly a decade to search out and record all the information assembled here. I must admit I was intrigued and challenged considerably—an experience that future generations can continue to enjoy since many mysteries remain for further research.

My hope is that future descendants of the Guzevicius/ Gustaff, Kubilius, Matusevicius, and Sierant/Shierant families will have some interest to learn about their ancestors' difficulties, hopes, joys, and tragedies as they arrived in the new world. I also hope that other readers may be inspired by the example of these courageous voyagers who started new lives and learned new ways but brought their traditions with them and added them to the cultural mix in their new land. Our forebears who left the old country never met with their parents in this world again. Their farewells were forever.

When immigrants arrived in America in the late 19th and early 20th centuries, they encountered many problems with their new lives. They looked to each other for help in adjusting to the difficulties that existed. Christian churches were founded in different ethnic communities and Catholic clergy helped ease the challenge of adjusting to American life.

Immigrants believed they brought wealth to the United States. Actually they did not bring wealth in their baggage. When they arrived they were penniless and in debt. But their real wealth existed in their skills, trades, and especially in their willingness to work, even in the lowliest jobs.

Many immigrants from Poland and Lithuania were engaged to work with mules and rats in the underground coal mining jobs. Cleanliness did not exist, and food had to be eaten with dirty hands and faces. Many miners developed "black lung" (anthrasilicosis, or "miner's asthma") from the coal dust they had to breathe. The meager wages they received for their hard work went toward paying the excessive prices they were charged for food in the stores that were built and run by the owners of the mines.

In spite of their difficulties, these immigrants worked hard to pursue the American dream for themselves and their families. Although many "native-born" Americans considered the new immigrants inferior, they should have remembered that every American, without exception, is either an immigrant or the descendant of immigrants. It is just these immigrants, wave on wave, who have made this country the colorful and always fascinating place it is today.

Prologue

I never realized how important it was that I write this book until my husband, Albert, and I returned from our visit to Lithuania in the year 1992. As descendants of emigrants from Lithuania and Poland we had long wished to visit our families' homeland, but during the years of Communist rule, this had been impossible. Now, at last, Communism had fallen in the Eastern European countries. Lithuania was free, the exiles were returning to their homeland, and we could meet with relatives again.

There was a need to bring Lithuanian people forward to meet the challenges and changes in a world unknown and unfamiliar to them after subjugation to a Soviet domination that had closed and sealed the borders of their country to visitors, families, and friends for fifty years (1941 to 1991).

From February to December, 1992, we taught English as a Second Language at Siauliai Pedagogical Institute, now known as Siauliai University, to students preparing to become teachers of

". . . UNTIL MY HUSBAND, ALBERT, AND I RETURNED
FROM OUR VISIT TO LITHUANIA . . . ."
The author, looking through border fence into Poland

"BY SHEER GOOD FORTUNE,
WE HAD THUS MADE CONTACT WITH RELATIVES . . . ."
Domicele, Liudgirdas, and his wife, Jurate

English in the prevailing elementary and secondary school system.

During our stay a local newspaper published an article
about us as the first volunteer teachers to come to Siauliai. A few
days later, to our astonishment, we received a visit from someone
who had seen the article and realized he was Albert's cousin! He
told us that his name was Liudgirdas Guzevicius, and that he was
the son of Albert's uncle Vladas, who had stayed behind in Lithuania when Albert's father emigrated to America nearly eighty
years before. By sheer good fortune, we had thus made contact
with relatives in this faraway place that our ancestors had left so
long ago.

Liudgirdas and his family brought us up to date on lives of
family members, deceased and living. We traveled by car along
roads that past generations had labored over by horse and wagon.
We visited the farms and homes where Albert's parents were born
and where they lived their early lives.

"THE SPINNING WHEEL AND THE BUTTER CHURN . . . HAD NOT BEEN
DESTROYED."

The author, Leona Gustaff; Domicele Guzeviciene

". . . THE BUILT-IN TILE STOVE [WAS] USED BY ALBERT'S GRANDMOTHER . . . ."

Domicele's modern cookware on the age-old stove in the birth home of Juozas Guzevicius

The spinning wheel and the butter churn, even the built-in tile stove used by Albert's grandmother, had not been destroyed. We saw the barn that had housed the cows, pigs, horses, and other animals. The same well into which Albert's ancestors had plunged buckets to be filled gave us fresh water. I noted that the view over the many acres of land owned by the family was expansive and beautiful, reaching across the border into Poland.

We met with Domicele, Liudgirdas's mother and Albert's aunt. Her husband, Albert's uncle Vladas, was not there. He had passed away many years earlier, unable to withstand the torture he received in the prisons of the Soviet *gulag*.

Domicele was thin and tiny, her face covered with deep wrinkles from the wind that blows often and sharp in the northern part of the world. I can still remember the growth on the left side of her right foot. It was aching red, about an inch in diameter, and it protruded just below the big toe. Her foot was white and

"The same well . . . which Albert's ancestors [used] . . . gave us fresh water."

The well on the Guzevicius farm

"... EXPANSIVE AND BEAUTIFUL, REACHING ACROSS THE BORDER INTO
POLAND."
The view of Poland from Guzevicius farm

wrinkled in contrast to the red bunion. Medical attention for bunions was rare in her part of the country. She could not wear shoes and was barefoot. Nevertheless, in spite of her seventy-five years she was spry and moved quickly.

Domicele and I lay comfortably on the cool grass under the hot sun talking to each other. Instead, I should say, she was talking, I was listening. Her story spoke volumes about the ordeal of Lithuania in the decades of Soviet oppression.

"It was fifty years ago," she began. "The Soviet government of Russia had taken over our land. They wanted to starve the initiative and leadership from the people of our country so that we would not have the strength to fight back. Our knowledgeable and educated people were exiled to Siberia or jailed. Since my husband, Vladas, was a teacher, an intellectual, I knew that they would come for him. The soldiers of the Red Army broke into our home in the middle of the night, and jamming guns into his ribs forced him into the carriage which transported him to the jail in the outskirts of the village. The Soviet soldiers claimed he was making serious accusations against the regime that was in power."

As she spoke I looked to the left at the rambling structure that was her home, the birth home of Juozas, my husband's father. A pathway of colorful stones ran to the front door, with flowers

"A PATHWAY OF COLORFUL STONES RAN TO THE FRONT DOOR . . . ."
Chickens pose in front of the birth home of Juozas Guzevicius, Albert's father

". . . NEARBY, WE COULD HEAR THE MOOING OF THE COW . . . ."
Domicele in front of the old barn at the Guzevicius homestead

blooming on both sides. Chickens and geese had escaped from behind a rough picket fence and were trotting back and forth paying no attention to the children who were playing on the ground not far away. From the old barn nearby, we could hear the mooing of the cow that would give us fresh milk to drink a little later.

Behind us and some distance from the house was the wooden outhouse. There were some new planks on the exterior, but I could see that it was quite old and needed renovation. There was no bathroom in the house in which Domicele lived.

As Domicele continued her story, she related how Soviet soldiers came again in the middle of the night and awakened her and her children from a restless sleep. "I was concerned that this would happen," she said, "but I had no control over it and could not avoid it."

The unwelcome visitors told her to collect whatever she thought would be needed for a long trip. "Be ready to leave when we return," she was ordered. Alone, her husband in jail, with no knowledge of her destination, she was frightened. Nevertheless, Domicele demanded to know what the charges were against her.

"Shooting and killing five members of the Soviet intelligence," she was told.

"How could this be?" she asked. "I have never held a gun in my hands."

"We have proof," they answered. "Your neighbors have reported you."

She then realized that, in order to protect themselves from the Soviet Terror and give themselves a chance to survive, her neighbors had fabricated a false denunciation. Sadly this was a common occurrence under Stalin's regime.

Domicele gathered all the food she could find in the house, and made sure she took potatoes and wheat. She packed the quilts she had spent many hours sewing. They would keep her children warm. Tautvyda, her two-year-old, was spending the night with a cousin in a neighboring village and so escaped deportation. Domicele was unhappy to be separated from her little daughter but was pleased that Tautvyda would not have to go to a strange and foreign land. Her cousin would take good care of Tautvyda. Domicele's two sons, Liudgirdas and Gintautas, ages four and

"KOSTAS AND JUOZAS . . . HAD BEEN *PARTISANAS* [(LITHUANIAN FREEDOM FIGHTERS)] . . . DURING WORLD WAR II."

Kostas, Albert, Leona, and Juozas

six, would have to go with her. She could not leave them behind alone.

❖

Domicele's exile in Siberia lasted many years. Unlike millions of others sent there by the Soviet regime, she survived the cold and hardship. Through her forced labor, Domicele helped start a community in Siberia. After Stalin's death in 1953, she, like many other surviving deportees, was allowed to leave. She returned to Lithuania to rebuild her shattered home and family.

Many of the exiles to Siberia died there from the unspeakable cold, starvation, and the slave-labor conditions forced upon them by their merciless Soviet captors. Their bodies were interred in the inhospitable earth of Siberia. Later, many of the exiles who did survive tried their best to find the graves of their relatives and friends who had perished in Siberia, in order to bring the bodies back to be reburied in the original homeland. Sadly, it was often impossible to find the graves.

Other relatives of Domicele—including Tautvyda Kriauciuniene, Liudgirdas's sister; Gintautas Guzevicius, his brother; and Laima Uzdaviniene, daughter of Stasys Guzevicius—also recounted to us the atrocities committed upon them by the Communists.

I have written at length about the harrowing exile to Siberia of Laima and her family in the journal *Bridges*, Volume 23, Issue 5, June 1999.

❖

Besides these relatives in the Guzevicius family, we also met with Kostas and Juozas Kubilius and their families. Kostas and Juozas, my husband's cousins on his mother's side, had been *partisanas* in Lithuania during World War II.

Partisanas (Lithuanian freedom fighters) formed a guerilla movement of men and women that carried on military missions attacking Soviet targets. Henry L. Gaidis, in his *History of the Lithuanian Military Forces in World War II, 1939-1945*, writes:

> A typical partisan unit consisted of volunteers from a particular area. The size of the unit was determined by the make-up of the geographical location, and the local population determined the unit's ability to hide and sustain itself in the field. Small, four to six man units could exist in a bunker-like formation on a farm, but larger units required a large forest area to hide in and allow for free movement unseen by the Soviets . . . .
>
> The war definitely delayed the Sovietization of Lithuania and took the lives of thousands of the [Soviet] enemy. Still, in a greater sense the partisans gave the nation the will to resist, and demonstrated to the world that the Lithuanian people were totally opposed to Soviet occupation. The partisans not only demonstrated the will of the people but proved the fact by being willing to lay down their lives for freedom.*

These stories about Albert's and my stay in Lithuania, our meetings with relatives, and the relatives' stories about hardships

---

*Henry L. Gaidis, *A History of Lithuanian Military Forces in World War II, 1939-1945* (Chicago: Lithuanian Research & Studies Center, Inc., and Vydunas Fund, Inc., 1998), pp. 268, 276.

of the Soviet era form the background for the present book. In this book, I have not written further about the tragic Soviet years, since all of our immigrant ancestors had left for the United States long before.

It was not my fortune to meet any of my mother's relatives while Albert and I were in Lithuania, nor did we have an opportunity to visit Poland where we might have located relatives on my father's side. Nevertheless, our meetings with Albert's relatives inspired in me a wish to write the stories of as many of our immigrant ancestors as I could. This book is the result. It tells about members of the Guzevicius, Kubilius, and Matusevicius families that brought our Lithuanian heritage to America.

I have also added the story of Jan and Ana Sierant, my father's parents, who had similar experiences coming to America from Poland (specifically from Galicia, an old region that includes what are now parts of southern Poland and western Ukraine).

Acknowledgments

I f this book is to be successful it will owe much to the interest and work put into it by Robert Randolph, my daughter Frances's husband, who is a trained historian of Eastern Europe and an experienced author and editor. It could not have reached its final form without him. He has edited my words with meticulous care and has guided me in the intricacies of publishing a book, an area in which I have had no expertise. I am truly thankful to him.

My cousin Albina Turowski Wegrzyn told me of reminiscences she had heard from her mother Mary, first child of my grandparents Ana and Jan Sierant. Albina's tale is the beginning of this narrative.

I received Ana Sierant's photo from my cousins Pauline Leones and Ann Shimmin, Jan and Ana's granddaughters by their second daughter, Katherine, when Albert and I visited Detroit, Michigan, in 1991. No photo of my grandfather Jan seems to exist.

I am also very grateful to Viktor Kubilius, nephew of Ona Guzeviciene. Since Viktor lived in Lithuania for many years before he emigrated to the United States, he was able to tell me, first hand, many impressions about the manner of living in the Guzevicius family while Juozas (Joe) and Ona (Anna/Annie) lived in the old world.

Elinor Marcel, daughter of Margaret Valatkiene, Ona Guzeviciene's sister, had many clear memories of the early years her mother, Margaret, and aunt Ona spent in Boston, Massachusetts. I wish to thank her for sharing them with me.

Vince Kaminski, grandson to Ciuty (grandma Ona Matuseviciene's sister Rose), gave me the information that the two sisters had entered the United States at the Baltimore port of entry.

My sister Irene, and my brothers Francis and Walter, shared with me their memories, which reinforced and supplemented mine in many helpful ways.

As I searched the C. Burr Artz Central Library in Frederick, Maryland, Mary Mannix, Archivist, and Mary Cramer, Branch Manager, found pertinent information and arranged for me to receive materials from other libraries.

The staff at the library in Mount Carmel, Pennsylvania, located information for me about that town where so many of the people in this book lived so much of their lives.

David Neimeyer, a family friend and a professional genealogist, graciously provided consultation and lent from his personal library reference books that helped guide our research and writing.

David Dubick, administrator of the Eckley Miners' Village Museum in Hazleton, Pennsylvania, gave permission to photograph, at the Museum, artifacts and illustrations from the Sierant and Matusevicius era, and to use those photographs in this book.

Suzanne Vastine-Smith, Prothonotary at Northumberland County Courthouse in Sunbury, Pennsylvania, answered my requests for birth and naturalization documents patiently. Lucille Shierant, my nephew Richard's wife, who works at the Sunbury courthouse, was instrumental in getting the information from the Courthouse quickly.

Upon a visit to the Church of Our Lady in Mount Carmel, Pennsylvania, my husband and I encountered Christina Joraskie, the church secretary, who searched the church files to discover from where in Galicia Jan and Ana departed for their journey to America.

Thomas Hollowak, Director, and Ann C. House, Collection Librarian, of the Steamship Historical Society of America at the Langsdale Library at the University of Baltimore, gave my husband and me information about ships used by immigrants to the United States. Most importantly, Ms. House located and sent us a photo of the ship *Bluecher*, on which Juozas Guzevicius traveled to America.

My daughter Ronni's husband Arthur Wehrhahn, Film Vault Manager for the Museum of Modern Art at the Film Preservation Center in Pennsylvania, introduced me to many tales about the beginning of film making and its historical significance.

Frank Cimino, a resident of Mount Carmel, Pennsylvania, sent me pertinent information about the early theaters in the town. Jake Betz, editor of the *Mount Carmel Item*, gave me permission to use information from his newspaper, specifically about the opening of the Victoria Theater.

Tom Kutz, a tourism expert, sent me copies of historic photographs of Mount Carmel and surrounding areas.

Dick Brani, a rare book dealer in Culpepper, VA, deserves special thanks for providing us with vital bibliographical information that we were unable to obtain anywhere else. Mr. Brani went out of his way to dig a book out of his collection, and then to search through the entire book to find the needed page reference, all in response to a frantic phone call from a perfect stranger. For this gracious act, the author and editor are sincerely grateful.

My friends Hilda Davis and Norma Chapman, writers of poetry and fiction, and my daughter Ronni, writer of fiction and non-fiction, spent many hours editing my fledgling original works as I started my quest into the lives of my ancestors.

My other children, Fran, Joan, and Joe, and their spouses read and commented on each story as it was written. They were a great help.

John and Yvonne White and many friends from Frederick, Maryland, gave me encouragement when they listened to my tales of mystery and aroused curiosity as I unearthed each new discovery. They helped me unravel snarls that seemed inexplicable.

I am grateful to my friend Dagmar Kolarik for reviewing and helping to format the recipes.

Debbie Gustaff Lynch, granddaughter of Juozas Guzevicius, prepared initial designs for the book cover. I am happy and thankful that she took the time and effort to help make this book more attractive and appealing.

Matthew Randolph, my grandson, spent many valuable hours first building and then maintaining the two computers that Albert and I used in creating this book, making sure that they would perform safely, quickly, and totally. Matthew played an even more crucial role at the end of the book's preparation, by identifying, acquiring, mastering, and finally using, with artistic skill, state-of-the-art graphic design software to lay out the book's pages, illustrations, and cover, and to produce the computer files that were then given to the printer to use in making the actual printing plates. Thank you Matthew!

The Soros Foundation in New York City contributed to the costs of our trip to Lithuania. The foundation's staff furnished valuable information and helped my husband and me to receive many educational materials to take with us.

My husband, Albert, has been my partner in all the experiences and research that led to this book. We traveled together to Lithuania, and to archives and museums in the United States. He spent much time organizing and filing all information requested, received, investigated, and reviewed, and for this I am very grateful. It was he who entered all our family history data into a computer database, and prepared cartographic information, from which then other computer software was used to produce the family-tree illustrations and maps that appear in this book. Albert encouraged me, made many profitable and useful suggestions, and most of all endured patiently all the months and years I devoted to this project. Without his participation and support, this book literally would not have been possible.

I am indebted to all. Each of them made my work easier and more complete. Nevertheless, I'm sure there is still much more to be uncovered about the family history, as about immigration history generally. Perhaps, in the future, a descendant will add more information to the stories of the Guzevicius/Gustaff, Kubilius, Matusevicius, and Sierant/Shierant families.

Note on Names

Lithuanian family names take different endings according to the gender and marital status of the person named, typically -ius for males, -iute for unmarried females, and -iene for married females. Thus Kubilius, Kubiliute, and Kubiliene are the same family name, simply different gender forms.

Many of the people discussed in this book changed their names when they arrived in the United States and in some cases later. Many had nicknames, both in Lithuanian and in English. Some common given names (e.g., "Ona") belonged to several different people in the story, inviting confusion. To make matters even more bewildering, by sheer coincidence two of the Onas (Matuseviciene and Guzeviciene) had sisters named Magdalena (married names Salaseviciene and Valatkiene), each of whom Americanized her name to Margaret!!

The author has tried hard to help the reader keep everything straight. For each individual at each point in time, the author has endeavored to use the name(s) by which the person was most commonly known at that time. The reader may find it easier to keep track of "who's who" by observing the running titles at the tops of pages, which indicate which family and often which individual is being discussed. Most of the people whose stories are told here can be found in the four genealogical charts (family trees) that are included at the end of the book.

For the eight principal characters in our drama (the four couples whose stories are told in Books One through Four), Table 1 lists all the names by which each person was known at various times in his or her life. In each case, the names shown in **bold** are the ones by which they are usually referred to here.

Finally, for the sake of any English-speaking readers who may be unfamiliar with pronunciation in Lithuanian, Polish, or other non-English languages, Table 2 lists a number of names and other words in those languages which are used in this book, with a simple guide to the pronunciation of each.

Table 1 - "DRAMATIS PERSONAE"

Legal Name	Name Late in Life: Among Family and Friends	Earlier or Variant Names	Birth Name	Dates	Relationship to Author
John Sherant	**Jan Sierant**	Joanne	Jan Sierant	c. 1869-1917	Father's father
Ana Sierant	**Ana Sierant**	Boder (1st marriage)	Ana Cieciwa	1859-1918	Father's mother
Martin Matusevicz	**Martinas Matusevicius**	Matusevich	Martinas Matusevicius	1875-1924	Mother's father
Ona Matusevicz	**Ona "Annie" Matuseviciene**	Matusevich, Matusevicius	Ona Malinauskaite	1873-1941	Mother's mother
Joseph Guzievyc	**Juozas "Joe" Guzevicius**		Juozas Guzevicius	1892-1975	Husband's father
Ona Guzievyc	**Ona "Anna/Annie" Guzeviciene**	Guzevicius	Ona Kubiliute	1890-1958	Husband's mother
Walter Shierant	**Walter "Wally" Shierant**		Ladislaus Sierant	1895-1966	Father
Veronica Shierant	Veronica **"Verna" Shierant**		Veronika Matuseviciute	1899-1972	Mother

Table 2 - PRONUNCIATION GUIDE

Name/word	Pronunciation	Name/word	Pronunciation
Ana	AH-nah	Juozas	YOH-zahs
Anele	ah-NEH-leh	Jurgis	YUR-gihs
Antanas	ahn-TAH-nahs	Kalinauskaite	kah-lih-NOW-skai-teh
Bazyte	bah-ZEE-teh	Katrina	kah-TREE-nah
Blazis	BLAH-zihs	Kielbasa	KEEL-bah-sah
Boder	BOH-der	Kobylis	koh-BEE-lihs
boilo	BOY-loh	Koncius	KOHN-chus
Budzeikaite	buhd-zay-KAI-teh	Kostas	KOHS-tahs
Chikotas	chih-KOH-tahs	Kubilius	kuh-BIH-lee-us
Cieciwa	chin-CHEE-va	Kubiliute	kuh-bih-LYOO-teh
Ciuty	CHUH-tee	Ladislaus	LAH-dis-loss
Damusis	dah-MUH-shis	Laima	LAI-mah
Domicele	doh-mih-TSEH-leh	Lithuania	lih-thu-AH-nee-ah
Galicia	gah-LEE-tsee-ah	Liudvikas	LUHD-vih-kahs
Gintautas	GIN-tow-tahs	Magdalena	mahg-dah-LEH-nah
Guzeviciene	guh-ZA-vih-cheh-neh	Magde	MAHG-deh
Guzevicius	guh-ZA-vih-chus	Magdyte	mahg-DEE-teh
Hilarium	hih-LEH-ree-um	Marija	mah-REE-yah
Jokubas	yoh-KOO-bahs	Martinus	mahr-TEE-nuhs
Jonas	YOH-nahs	Matuleviciute	mah-tu-la-vih-CHOO-teh
Josefina	yoh-seh-FEE-nah	Matusevicz	ma-tu-SEH-vich
Jozef	YO-zef	Moszczenica	mosh-chen-NEE-tsah
Jule	YOO-leh	Novitsky	noh-VIHT-skee

Key: a/man; ah/father; ai/kite; au/out; ay/way; ch/chip; ee/cheese; eh/let;
ey/they; g/get; ih/sip; oh/lone; oo/zoo; ow/now; th/thin; u/put; uh/dud;
ye/yes; zh/vision

Table 2 - PRONUNCIATION GUIDE (Continued)

Name/word	Pronunciation	Name/word	Pronunciation
Ona	OH-nah	Stanislaus	STAH-nihs-loss
Pajaujis	pa-YOW-yihs	Stasys	stah-SEES
partisanas	par-tah-ZAH-nahs	Tautvyda	towt-VEE-dah
Pranas	PRAH-nahs	Turowski	tu-ROFF-skee
Punskas	PUHN-skahs	Uzdaviene	UHZH-dah-veh-neh
pyraga	pee-RAH-gah	Valanciunas	vah-lahn-CHOO-nahs
Rodwakowski	rohd-vah-KOFF-skee	Valatkiene	vah-laht-KYEH-neh
Rudamina	ruh-dah-MIH-nah	Viktor	VIHK-tohr
ruta	ROO-tah	Vincas	VIHN-sahs
Salasavicius	sah-lah-SA-vih-chus	Vladas	VLAH-dahs
Shierant	SHAI-rant	Vytautas	VEE-tow-tahs
Siary	see-AH-ree	Wegrzyn	VEH-grih-zhihn
Siauliai	SHOW-lay	Zovoda	zho-VOH-dah
Sierant	sher-AHNT	Zuikaite	zoo-ey-KAI-teh

Key: a/man; ah/father; ai/kite; au/out; ay/way; ch/chip; ee/cheese; eh/let; ey/they; g/get; ih/sip; oh/lone; oo/zoo; ow/now; th/thin; u/put; uh/dud; ye/yes; zh/vision

Note on Sources

Most of the information used in writing this book came from the author's and her husband's own recollections and from conversations with older family members. Many details were obtained from public records (birth and death certificates, U.S. census records, and the like). In a few cases, gaps in the documentary record have obliged the author to engage in imaginative reconstruction, based on published information about the experiences of other immigrants to the United States during the late nineteenth century. The author has included information about sources wherever possible throughout the text, and where portions of the narrative are reconstructions, has indicated this. Photographs for which no source reference is indicated were obtained from the family's own collection or from a private source who preferred to remain anonymous.

To compose and assemble these stories, my husband and I searched church and county records, made numerous visits to the National Archives in Washington, D.C., and pored over the U.S. census records for the years 1900, 1910, and 1920, all the relevant years that had been opened to the public by the time we were doing our research.

Jan and Ana's information was the most difficult to locate. Most of the bare facts that we learned about them came from documents we obtained from the Prothonotary, or Chief Clerk of the Court of Law, at Sunbury, Pennsylvania. We sent correspondence to Polish churches in Brooklyn and other parts of New York City, where we knew they had lived before settling in Pennsylvania, but always we received the reply that nothing was unearthed. As a result, we don't know where or when they were married.

The stories about Juozas and Ona Guzevicius are from the perspectives of my husband Albert and his years living with them. He was frank and honest and searched his mind for his best recollections.

I wrote the stories of Martinas and Ona Matusevicius and of Walter and Verna Shierant through memories of my life with them. I have endeavored to be truthful. To supplement my recollections I studied many photographs and enjoyed conversations with my siblings and with my cousin George Sierant. I have also interviewed other friends and relatives still living.

Book One

Jan and Ana Sierant

REQUIEM

Where the front porch
touches the sidewalk
families move
to the tempo of men
who carve black gold
from the bowels of the earth
groan, crumble
colliery sirens roar
Kulpmont - two blasts - pause
Locust Summit - three blasts - pause.

Homes unprotected, children untended,
confused women
rush with fears they may find
father, husband, son, brother,
twisted body crushing fire
calls for water or
deep in the wet and moldy
only a memory - not a living man.

LS/G

Chapter One

Ana Cieciwa

The stones are far apart. In fact, they're in two different cemeteries. Chiseled crude letters and numbers on one stone are: Jan Sierant - Died April 18, 1917. The other, barely discernable because of the ravages of time, tells us: Ana Sierant - Died April 27, 1918.

Ana and Jan were my grandparents, but I never knew them. I was six months old when the earth was dug to bury Ana's body. In the summer of 1989 my husband, Albert, and I visited my cousin Albina in Detroit, Michigan, and heard their story.

"They had come from the old country to settle in America about 1890," she began. "Jan came alone, but Ana was accompanied by her son Jozef. They traveled steerage, below deck, huddled together with masses of men, women and children, everyone hoping to make better lives for themselves in their chosen country.

"Ana Cieciwa—her family name," Albina continued, looking to see if we understood, "was married in Poland at a young age to Jozef Boder, a young man who lived on a neighboring farm. Soon they had three children. Jozef, the first born, was followed by twin boys."

My cousin interrupted her story to say, "Don't ask me the names of the twins, I just don't know."

"Please listen," she went on. "There was a time that sickness was rampant in Poland and the twins became ill. The need for medication was immediate, and Ana begged her husband to run as quickly as possible to the doctor to purchase it. He had to walk a great distance through stormy weather, but the urgency could not be put off. His neighbors along the way warned him to be careful. He ran until he reached the brook where he discovered that the rushing stream had washed the bridge away. The raging waters picked him up as he attempted to cross, and carried him to

"JAN CAME ALONE, BUT ANA WAS ACCOMPANIED BY HER SON JOZEF."

Ana Sierant, c. 1917

(photo courtesy of Pauline Leones and Ann Shimmin)

his death. Without the medication, the twins joined their father."

This much Albina told my husband and me about my grandmother's life in Poland. To realize why she came to America with Jozef, her remaining son, I searched through the archives in Washington, D.C., and studied the history of the immigrants of that era.

My father, Walter, who was Ana and Jan's son, once told me that his parents were from Galicia, a part of Poland believed to be the poorest region in Europe. Work was scarce and there was very little food in their homes. They read advertisements about the wonderful opportunities in America and were encouraged by their families and friends to emigrate there.

Galicia was an area in southeastern Poland near Krakow, under the rule of the Austro-Hungarian Empire. Adjoining Slovakia to the South, Galicia covered the northern slopes of the Carpathian mountains and the adjoining plains, stretching from Krakow to beyond Lvov, in what is now Ukraine.

Galicia had a high birth rate and could not produce enough food to sustain its inhabitants. "In the twenty-five years before the First World War, more than two million people left Galicia for good . . . . Most took the ship from Hamburg for America, joining the ceaseless tide of Europe's weary and oppressed who passed through Ellis Island on their way to the mines of Pennsylvania or to the Frontier lands of the Midwest."*

In the late 1880s women in the Polish countryside worked either on the land of their family farms or as servants to neighboring farm owners. We surmise that Ana's family was poor, and Ana probably worked for a family near her home. She would have helped with the children, as well as done housework, for wages paid in *zlotys*, which translated at that time into twenty-five American cents a day. The price of one pair of shoes would have been her entire salary for two months.

Ana may have seen leaflets distributed by American owners of development programs for railroads and mines, which described an abundance of opportunities for work in their land. Some Galicians who had braved the daring adventure of traveling over the ocean to America returned to tell stories about a wealthy

*Norman Davies, *God's Playground, a History of Poland* (New York: Columbia University Press, 1982), vol. 2, p. 147.

land with freedom to speak your own thoughts and practice your religious faith without political or religious tyranny.

Railroads had arrived in Poland, and steamships were replacing sailing ships, lessening the voyage to the new country from three months to ten days . The price of the "ship-card" (ticket for passage) was twelve dollars, which Ana could afford if she sold all her possessions.

We read that families who had arrived in the United States of America years earlier and were already rewarded with the riches of the country were in need of young women to help them with housework and child care. My grandma was probably approached through friends, or may have answered an advertisement seeking servants, and was offered a position as maid to a family in New York City.

It is also possible that she was greeted at the port of entry by a relative. As we searched the archives, we found the name Cieciwa among the residents of New York in those days. Correspondence from St. Stanislaus Church in New York City informed us of Hilarium Cieciwa's marriage to Mariam Bindas on May 18, 1890, both residing in Yonkers, New York. Hilarium had also emigrated from Galicia. (At this time we don't know if there is any relationship between Hilarium and Ana.)

As Ana prepared for her trip she probably could not bear to leave her handmade linens and blankets behind, and she gathered them together with her meager supply of clothing into a large cloth bag. She possibly also packed smoked sausage and dark rye bread which she feared would not be available in America. She wore two petticoats, two dresses, her newest jacket, a kerchief on her head, and a shawl over her shoulders. She put two suits of clothes on her son to eliminate some baggage. Her remaining zlotys she sewed into the hem of her jacket.

At the port of embarkation, before boarding the ship, all passengers were vaccinated and disinfected. Ana's hair was combed carefully and searched for lice, which could have carried typhus. Men and boys had their hair cut very short.

The trip was not easy. Ana and her son undoubtedly traveled steerage, the lowest level of the ship, which, we read, was crammed with hundreds of passengers. It held one bath area for men at one end, another for women at the other end, and offered little privacy. It's conceivable that Ana had seasickness from the rolling motion of the ship, and did not see daylight or feel the healing warmth of the sun until she reached her destination.

❖

In 1884, at the age of twenty-five, tired and physically worn out, Ana arrived in her new country with her son Jozef, who was six years old. According to cousin Albina, the port of entry was "Castle Garden", the immigration center in New York City at that time. Here arriving immigrants were examined by officials who poked objects into their eyes and down their throats looking for possible infections. Through interpreters the immigrants were asked endless questions: "Do you have relatives in America? Are you going outside of New York? How much money do you have? Where will you work? Was your passage paid by yourself or by a charitable organization?"

If Ana had not been greeted by a relative, she probably went directly to the family that had hired her. She started her chores at once. Although her wages were small, they were much larger than she had received in her native country. The family treated her well, but assigned her arduous tasks.

My friend Ellen told me this story:

> "My grandmother's sister, Norah, came from Ireland to work as a maid for a family which, she said, was very good to her. One day they bought a bathtub for the house. 'Do not use this bathtub. It's only for the family,' Norah was told. The family visited relatives every Saturday night. When they had left on one of those excursions, Norah's curiosity could not be put aside. She poured bucketfuls of hot water into the tub. Gingerly she put her toes in first and then little by little the rest of her body. Her employers came home earlier than expected and found Norah in the tub splashing the water over herself, taking the first tub bath of her life. She was dismissed from her position, but was soon employed by another family, and eventually met a sturdy Irish lad and married him."

❖   ❖   ❖

It is possible that by 1889 Ana had saved enough money to rent an apartment in a tenement building in Brooklyn. Later, we know (from Albina's testimony) that Ana supported herself by housing immigrants from Poland and other European countries. From records at the Library of Congress in Washington, D.C., we found the name "Ana Boda" living in Brooklyn at that time, at 98 Debevoise Street. There is a possibility this is the surname of Ana Cieciwa's husband who had perished in Galicia. Boda is the closest spelling to Boder, the surname used by Ana's son for his entrance into the military and for the carving on his headstone. We could never discover the surname Boder in our early searches for information concerning Ana and her son.

Oscar Handlin in his book *The Uprooted* describes the apartments of immigrant families:

> Each suite in this six-story structure had three rooms; but the rooms were smaller (4x11, 8x7, and 8x7 [sic]). There were gas lights in the halls, but the water closets were in sheds in the alleys. And well over half the rooms had no windows at all.*

Ana probably became a devout member of the Polish Roman Catholic church near her home and enrolled Jozef in the parochial school. This would have been a familiar and welcome support to her, since she had practiced her faith with intense ardor before she crossed the Atlantic.

The church would have become a social center where she could attend parties and dances, and meet friends of the same language and culture. Possibly at the church she might have become acquainted with the Felician Sisters, a Polish teaching order that, we are told, encouraged Polish immigrants to speak English and become American patriots while retaining their Polish traditions. Through searching the history of Polish immigrants to America we discovered that the Felician Sisters taught English in the Brooklyn area.

---

*Oscar Handlin, *The Uprooted* (Boston: Little Brown, 1990), p. 133.

It appears that Ana must have been determined that her children know the English language very well. Evidently she continued to add words to her English vocabulary and would not speak her native language to the family, judging from the fact that my father and his siblings never learned to converse in Polish. Mary, the eldest, was the only one who knew the language. Mary also remarked to Albina that Ana, Mary's mother, spoke and wrote to her in English.

Mary and Ana corresponded with each other after Mary was married and moved to Detroit, Michigan. (She married John Theodore Turowski in St. Joseph's Church in Mount Carmel, Pennsylvania, on October 19, 1911.) Unfortunately, none of the letters Mary and Ana exchanged were saved.

Chapter Two

Jan Sierant

When Jan Sierant came to this country around 1889, he was probably about twenty years old. He was tall with a light complexion and a sturdy lean body. Cousin Albina describes him as handsome with a beautiful set of teeth. We have no information about why he left his native land but surmise that he could not support himself with the meager portion of land he had inherited from his parents.

Albina relates that when Jan Sierant arrived in his new country he moved into Ana's boarding house. He must have had difficulty getting work in New York since he could not speak English, but he could have been attracted to newspapers and signs on posts in the streets, advertising jobs available in the mines in Pennsylvania. We don't know if he realized that men working there were in constant danger from perilous working conditions and, if they were lucky enough to escape the cave-ins, most of them eventually would suffer from miner's asthma, a cause of early death.

Jan surely did not want to go to Pennsylvania without a wife. He probably longed for a home and family as he would have had in Poland. It's very likely that he asked Ana to go with him and promised he would be a good husband and work to support her well. We are told that in that era love was not a necessity, and marriages were arranged either by families or for convenience.

According to the 1910 census Ana was ten years older than Jan, but certainly she would have been an appealing marriage partner because there were very few women in America who could speak both Polish and English well. She, in turn, would have difficulty finding a husband since she was a widow with a child.

Although we have sent many letters to Polish churches in New York (Manhattan and Brooklyn), we could not determine where and when Jan and Ana were married. In 1890, a likely place for their wedding could have been Our Lady of Czestochowa Polish Roman Catholic Church in Brooklyn.

Wherever the wedding took place, Jan certainly must have been impressive in his Sunday-best suit with a store-bought white shirt and tie. Ana probably wore a long dress with sleeves to the wrists plus a stand-up collar, and bought a new pair of gloves and shoes for the important occasion. As Jan and Ana walked down the aisle, tall and dignified, they must have been a striking couple.

Ana's son, Jozef, twelve years of age at the time, may have given his mother away. Perhaps the boarders, Jan and Ana's friends, the Felician sisters, and the pastor attended a party in the social room of the church after the ceremony. They would have celebrated with gusto, singing old-country folk tunes and swinging and dancing to polkas played on an accordion by a Polish immigrant. On the other hand, Jan and Ana may have departed immediately to their destination—Pennsylvania and the coal mines.

Chapter Three

Pennsylvania

My husband, Albert, and I made many arduous visits to the National Archives in Washington, D.C. At the archives, we learned from the U.S. census of 1910 that Jan and Ana were living in Marion Heights, Pennsylvania, at 107 Claremont Street. At that time it probably was a "patch town," a tiny settlement consisting of just one or at most a few unpaved streets, lined with homes that were dilapidated shanties, in the shadow of a colliery. The mine owners who had built the houses for their workers charged extortionate rents for their use.

The company store where Ana was compelled by her husband's employer to buy all her groceries and other necessities stood at one end of the street, with prices at least 20% higher

"THE MINE OWNERS . . . CHARGED EXTORTIONATE RENTS FOR THEIR USE."

A "patch town" home for two families

(photo courtesy of Eckley Miners' Village Museum)

"BUYING WAS DONE ON 'TICK' . . . [AT THE COMPANY] STORE."
A typical company store in the Mount Carmel area

than those in nearby towns. Buying was done on 'tick' and was recorded in a book kept by the proprietor of the store. The beer hall was located at the other end of the street on which Jan walked home each day from the coal mine where he worked.

❖

We don't know for sure when Jan and Ana arrived in Pennsylvania, but it must have been between 1889, when Jan immigrated to America, and 1893, when we know their son Andrew (their second child) was born in Pittston, Pennsylvania. (Their first child, Mary, had been born in 1892, but we do not know where.) By 1895, the family evidently had moved to Willburton, Pennsylvania, judging from the fact that my father, Walter (their third child) was born there at that time. (My father was baptised Ladislaus, the Polish form of the name Walter.) In the 1900 census, we could not find any information, not even the name *Sierant*. However, as of 1901, when Jan registered his intention to become a naturalized citizen, he indicated that his intended place of settlement was Mount Carmel, Pennsylvania. From the 1910 census, we know that by then the family was living in Marion Heights, Pennsylvania.

❖

But we are getting ahead of the story. Some of these same documents provide information about Jan's earlier vital data—e.g., dates of birth, immigration, and marriage.

For instance, we received from the Northumberland County Prothonotary in Sunbury, Pennsylvania, information that on June 22, 1901, Jan registered for naturalization with two friends as witnesses who swore that Jan fulfilled the residency requirements. He had resided for more than five years within the limits and under the jurisdiction of the United States. For the past three years his intention had been to become a citizen of the United States. He renounced allegiance to Francis Joseph, Emperor of Austria, to whom he had formerly been a subject.

Jan wrote that he was born in Austria and was 31 years of age. He emigrated from Austria in 1885 and intended to settle in Mount Carmel, Pennsylvania. On the document the Prothonotary spelled his name *John Sherant*, but Jan signed, in script, *John Sierant*. It is possible that Jan pronounced his surname as Sherant, using the Polish pronunciation. Ana did not apply for naturalization, perhaps because women did not yet have the right to vote.

The 1910 census claims Jan Sierant was 41; married in 1890; place of birth, Galicia, Poland; subject of Austria; year of immigration 1889 [note that this differs from the date given in his naturalization papers, described above]; coal miner; can read and write in English; owns his own home at 107 Claremont Street, in Marion Heights, Pennsylvania.

❖

Jan and Ana lived in Marion Heights about twenty years and had six children in all: Mary, Andrew, Walter, George, Katherine (Kate), and Frank. Soon after birth each undoubtedly was baptized, and we know that in three cases (Walter, George, and Kate) the baptism took place at St. Joseph's Roman Catholic Church on Hickory Street in Mount Carmel, where Ana and Jan attended.

We surmise that Jan worked in the mines: hundreds of feet below sunlight; six days a week, ten hours a day; breathing un-

"JAN AND ANA LIVED IN MARION HEIGHTS ABOUT TWENTY YEARS AND HAD SIX CHILDREN."

Walter (Wally), George, Mary, (Mary's son and his wife), Andrew, Katherine (Katie), and Frank

"... ANA WORKED A LONG DAY ...."
Mothers and children pick coal by hand
(photo courtesy Eckley Miners' Village Museum)

healthy coal dust, prelude of 'black lung'. The poorly ventilated shafts were prone to explosions, floods, and fires. Strangely, rats were welcome companions. A buildup of deadly mine gas was not noticeable to a human being, but when rats began scurrying to leave the area quickly, the miners were alerted to the escaping vapors.

❖

Sunday, Jan rested. If he were not tired, he might play pinochle with the men at the beer hall or attend one of the many ball games held by the men of the 'patch towns.' The vigorous and noisy weddings and social parties that took place often must have been enjoyed by Jan and Ana. The accordionist was surely very popular, especially if his repertoire consisted of lively Polish music for the polka dancers.

In Hazleton, Pennsylvania, at Eckley Miners' Village Museum, which portrays the immigrant miners' life in the early

"IN WINTER THE STOVE GAVE HEAT TO WARM THE ROOM . . . ."
An early coal-fed stove, used to do laundry as well as for cooking
(photo courtesy Eckley Miners' Village Museum)

twentieth century, we deduced that Ana worked a long day in and around her home. She awoke at 5:00 a m , and by eight o'clock her husband and children were fed. She had to stoke the stove with coal and either rekindle the fire of the evening before or begin a new fire, and carry in water from the spring down the street. In winter the stove gave heat to warm the room as well as to cook the dinner. In summer the stove was dismantled and placed outside the home so that the family would not have to suffer the heat it generated.

Perhaps Ana had gotten the coal by picking it out from the "culm piles" (vast heaps of discarded coal screenings) near the mines. This was dirty, dangerous work but an important way of stretching a patch-town family's meager income.

Ana sewed clothing for the children and curtains for the home. A basket of articles for mending was never empty. Washing clothes and baking bread were chores to be done at least once or twice a week. In summer the potatoes and cabbage planted in the garden had to be tended.

In the fall, many hours were spent canning and storing food for the winter months. The road-dust and coal-dust had to be swept from the wood floors in the house many times every day.

In the *U.S. News* issue of August 28 to September 4, 1995, on page sixty, Mary McQuerry, who was 104 years old, wrote:

"A SIMPLE TASK LIKE LAUNDRY TOOK HALF A DAY . . . ."
Laundry had to be stirred as it was boiled in this large copper kettle
(photo courtesy Eckley Miner's Village Museum)

"MONDAYS WERE WASH DAYS. YOU SCRUBBED ON A BOARD . . . .
TUESDAY WAS IRONING DAY. THE IRONS WERE SIX OR SEVEN POUNDS."

Strong arms were needed to turn the crank of this wringer
(photo courtesy Eckley Miners' Village Museum)

Women's brutal job was housekeeping: A simple task like laundry took half a day from boiling the water to pulling the wash off the clothes line (frozen stiff, in winter). They knew their neighbors, helped each other without being asked and chatted on front porches in the evenings.

Mondays were wash days. You scrubbed on a board, then stirred the clothes in boiling water and then through two rinses and some bluing. Tuesday was ironing day. The irons were six or seven pounds. You heated them in the fireplace and the process took all day.

I did gardening the rest of the week. Sunday I rested. Before church, I'd catch a chicken and pin it to the ground under my foot. I'd pull its head off with my hands.

Chapter Four

Michigan

Ana Sierant's days were probably miserable. She must have yearned for her early life in Poland. The children gradually became adults and left home to pursue their own careers.

Andrew married Agatha (Aggie) Novitsky and moved to Chicago, Illinois; George followed Andrew to Chicago where he married Jeanette (Jenny) Furmanski. Frank also went to Chicago where he married Stella Furmanski. All three brothers became machine operators and worked at International Harvester.

Kate married George Leones in Melvindale, Michigan, and settled in Pittsburgh, Pennsylvania. (George Leones passed away August 7, 1922, and Kate later married George Bastas.) As stated earlier, Mary had married John Turowski in Mount Carmel, Pennsylvania. They settled in Detroit, Michigan.

"Ana, our grandmother, left Jan, our grandfather, and traveled by train to Detroit to stay with her daughter Mary, my mother," Albina told us. "Life was much easier for Ana. She enjoyed conversing with my mother every day, and even spoke her native Polish. Her greatest happiness was her ability to be at Mass each day, since the Catholic church was within walking distance from our home.

"Jan was not happy living alone. He missed Ana and his many active children. He decided to go to Detroit, also by train, to try a reconciliation with Ana. Ana refused to see him."

Albina remembered that our grandfather registered himself into a sanatorium for the poor, destitute, and alcoholics, named Eloise, in Westland, Michigan. It was closed and torn down about twenty years ago.

"Shortly after grandfather Jan arrived," my cousin continued as she recalled her mother's words, "our grandmother became very ill. The goiter on her throat, with which she suffered for many years, became overly large, and in the early twentieth century no cure was available for this illness. She rallied for a while but then went into delirium. In her hallucinations she began to call for her husband.

"My mother went to the sanatorium to see our grandfather. The director of the building had difficulty recognizing his name at first, but later recalled that John Sherant had passed away April 18, 1917." We could not get information concerning his death, but we are surmising that he died from 'black lung', the miners' disease.

Ana died April 27, 1918. According to the attending physician, Doctor Husband, the cause of death was Exapthalmic Goitre. Information received from the Director of the cemetery revealed to us that Ana was interred in Holy Cross Cemetery in Detroit, in Lot 35, Grave 365. No headstone exists.

After much searching we discovered that Jan was laid to rest in Eloise Cemetery, Lot 356. (*More information under Observations, later in this chapter.*)

❖

We never discovered why Ana left Jan. My cousin Ann Shimmin related to me that both her mother Kate and our aunt Mary, children of Ana and Jan, told her that their father Jan was an alcoholic. My recollection of stories related by my parents is that there were many alcoholics who became irrational and uncontrollable after imbibing whiskey, much of it homemade. Working in the mines was almost unbearable, and liquor was so easily obtainable that my grandfather Jan could have become an alcoholic. This may have been the reason he became a patient at Eloise, a sanatorium with a history of admitting alcoholics.

I have often wondered why our surname was not Polish sounding. During our search we met a Dr. Piotr (Peter) Sierant, who lives in Norwich, Connecticut. He had conducted a genealogical study of the Sierant name in Poland, where he met a friend who encountered the name Louis Sierant in documents from 1772.

This was the time of the Polish patriotic uprising against the country's Russian-dominated last king, Stanislaus August Poniatowski, one of Russian empress Catherine the Great's many lovers. The uprising, which began in 1768, was supported by France as a way to undermine its rival Russia. French "volunteers" came to Poland to help the uprising. Ultimately it did not succeed, and Poland was partitioned by Russia, Austria, and Prussia.

In 1772, records indicate that a marriage took place between Louis (Ludwig) Sierant and a Polish noblewoman. It is thought that Sierant was a French officer who came to the city of Pilsno, Poland, with a regiment led by either Duhamel de Precourt or Baron Viomenilla, both French commanders.

A son was born to the Sierants in 1773 whose godfather was a Count Rodwakowski. Three other sons were born. More research is needed to establish connections between Sierant families in Poland and the United States.

I began this tale by saying that the stones are far apart. I was wrong. Unfortunately, no headstones exist. I received my information about Jan and Ana from church, county, and census records; from recollections of the few words my father spoke about his family; and from cousin Albina's reminiscences.

Observations

Ann Shimmin, daughter of Kate, Jan and Ana's daughter, sent me an article from the *Detroit News* dated Sunday, November 1, 1998, about the forgotten cemetery at Wayne County Asylum in Westland, Michigan, called Eloise Mental Hospital.

According to the article, the land had recently gained the interest of developers. One caption reads: "An abandoned cemetery used by the Eloise mental hospital on an isolated patch of land near Michigan Avenue in Westland was rediscovered just a few years ago."

"But the overgrown property is untouchable since more than 7,100 nameless gravestones are hidden on the eastern edge of the lot, making it impossible to build upon it. Many of the records are lost and there is no way to know who's buried there."

Earlier we had sent correspondence to the Michigan Department of Community Health requesting a death certificate for Jan Sierant/Sherant/Shierant. They wrote back saying there was no record of his death. Albina had related to us that she heard her mother mention that her father passed away at Eloise.

Today, September 1, 2000, I read the *Detroit News* article more carefully and discovered there was a person named Frank Rembisz, director of the Wayne County Office of Aging, whose office was housed in the Kay Beard Building at Eloise. He was also the unofficial county historian. After a series of telephone calls I was speaking with him directly. He offered to look up the information. A few hours later I called back and received the following:

> Your grandfather's name is spelled 'Sherant'
> He came from Austria.
> He was listed as a laborer.
> Entered Eloise June 22, 1915.
> Died April 18, 1917.
> His lot is #356.
> At the time of death he was 50 years, 3 months, 24 days old.

As a result we have figured his birth date to have been January 25, 1867.

This raises many questions. Why did he enter Eloise? Was he an alcoholic? This was common at that time among immigrants. Was he insane? Schizophrenic? Why did our grandmother refuse to see him? Did he abuse her? The article mentions that mentally ill patients were separated from the other patients. This leads me to believe there also were normal patients there.

To talk about dates: According to his naturalization papers dated June 22, 1901, he was 31 at the time. This makes his birth date 1870. On the April 18, 1910, census he was 41. This makes his birth date 1869.

Addendum

In February 2002 my husband and I decided to make one more trip to Mount Carmel, Pennsylvania, the town in which my grandparents had settled. We thought we might be able to find some missing information if we made a personal visit.

Our initial plan was to go to St. Joseph's Polish Catholic Church rectory. Unfortunately, St. Joseph's Church had been closed a few years earlier, and all information had been sent to the Church of Our Lady, on Market Street.

When we arrived at the Church of Our Lady we were greeted by Christina Joraskie, secretary to the parish. We explained our needs, and she ushered us into a small room containing two oversized cabinets.

Ms. Joraskie reached for a large book of baptismal records. Together, she and I searched through the pages. We found the name Adalbertum (Wojciech) Sierant. The information on the paper was in Latin. The date on the certificate was 26 Aprilis, 1897. We recognized the birth date as that of George Sierant, son of Jan Sierant and Ana Cieciwa. This certificate, which the secretary copied for us, had eluded us from the beginning of the genealogy search, because the search had always been for the first name "George."

Later that evening, as I studied the old-fashioned handwriting on the certificate, I tried to decipher the words that appeared after Jan and Ana's names in the spaces marked *"ex loco"* ("from the place"). And suddenly I realized that one of the words was "Galicia".

Very excited I asked myself, "Could it possibly be one of the links to Jan and Ana's story that we've been searching for the past ten years?"

Robert Randolph, our daughter Frances's husband and editor of this book, later studied the old handwriting too and made out the following:

Ego infrascriptus baptizavi - Adalbertum (Wojciech)

natum - 26 Aprilis 1897
ex - Joanne Sierant
ex loco - Moszczenica, Gorlice, Galicia
et - Anna Cieciwa
ex loco - Siary, Gorlice, Galicia
Patrini fuerunt - Karol Niemice, Anna Garsa
(Translation below)*

We still questioned whether it was my uncle George on the certificate, so we contacted my cousin George Sierant (son of George Sierant the elder) at his home in Birmingham, Michigan. Cousin George informed us that his mother had told him that "George" was not really his father's baptismal name. But his mother did not know the name by which his father was baptized.

Cousin George also remarked that his mother maintained that according to Polish custom his father was called George because the date of his birth was either on St. George's feast day, or close to it. After some searching we learned that the feast day for St. George is April 23.

"Joanne Sierant" and "Anna Cieciwa" are very close to the spellings of my grandparent's names. My father had told me that my grandfather had come from Galicia. We were astounded! There could be no question! We had discovered the villages in Poland where Jan and Ana lived before they emigrated to the United States!

---

*I the undersigned baptized - Adalbert (Wojciech)
born - 26 April 1897
from [father] - Jan Sierant
from the place - Moszczenica, Gorlice, Galicia
and [mother] - Anna Cieciwa
from the place - Siary, Gorlice, Galicia
Godparents were - Karol Niemice, Anna Garsa

John (Joanne) Sierant emigrated from **Moszczenica, Gorlice, Galicia.**

Ana Cieciwa emigrated from **Siary, Gorlice, Galicia.**

Book Two

Martinas and Ona Matusevicius

RAIN (LITHUANIA 1992)

Liquid caresses my cheeks
Flows down to touch my tongue
Droplets turn me into a fish
Lietus, lietus, visada lietus.*
I'm beset by cold humidity
My skin swelters from frost
I skim the waves of the Baltic Sea.

Spoons of fluid vanish into clouds.
Midst a rainbow a battered sun
Limps to mend broken minds.
Trampled scents of birch trees rustle
Fractured sounds on tiny hills.
Racemes stretch out and drip
Bleeding hearts.

---

*Rain, rain, always rain.

LS/G

Chapter Five

Lithuania

Martinas and Ona Matusevicius were my grandparents. Verna, my mother, was their first child. One day while traveling with my mother in the family Ford through Merriam, the small town at the base of Merriam Mountain in Pennsylvania, I asked how she came to this country.

"I lived in one of those houses on the back street in Merriam when I first came to America. It's fixed up now, but it was a shanty when we lived here," she said. "My father came to America first. He worked in the colliery across the road for two years before he sent ship-cards to us so that my mother, my brother, and I could come here to live with him."

"I often wondered how grandpa came to the United States."

"He was sponsored by his friend, Mr. Pavis, who came earlier and worked in the mines."

"Mr. Pavis? That doesn't sound like a Lithuanian name."

"His name was Pajaujis in Lithuania. You know that everybody changed their names when they came to America. They were afraid they wouldn't get jobs with Lithuanian names. We

"HE WORKED IN THE COLLIERY . . . SO THAT [WE] COULD COME HERE . . . ."

The Locust Summit colliery was across the road from the "patch town" Merriam, Pennsylvania

even changed our first names. That's why I'm called Verna and not Veronika; my father, Martinas, is Martin; Ona, my mother, is Annie."

"Tell me about Mr. Pavis, mom," I asked.

"He and my father used to play together as children in the old country. They had lived not very far from each other. Because he wasn't married it was easy for him to come to the United States before my father did. He sent a ship-card to my father, and my father paid him back when he came here to live."

"I'd like to meet him. Please tell me where he is."

"I don't know where he is now. He saved a lot of money and returned to Lithuania to buy a farm. No one has ever heard from him since then. We don't know even if he's still alive. He helped many Lithuanians come to America, not only my father. I am not certain, but he may have sponsored Uncle Antanas (Anthony) Salasevicius, who possibly came to America on the same boat with my father. Uncle Antanas was the husband of my mother's sister, Rosie. He later sent ship-cards to his wife and their two children, Ona (Annie) and Anele (Nellie)."

Martinas Matusevicius, the father of my mother, Verna, was born in Rudamina, a village located in Southern Lithuania not far from the Polish border. In his Declaration of Intention to secure a Certificate of Naturalization, dated January 8, 1912, he states that he was born on the first day of November 1875. The 1910 census notes that he was 35 years of age at the time the census was taken. His parents were Andrew Matusevicius and Mary Pomonoskaite.

A small man, Martinas became a farmer in Lithuania. He never was educated, and although he gave some thought to it, he never dreamed he'd go to America.

In 1898 he married Ona Malinauskaite, whose parents farmed land close by. Martinas and Ona were wed in a Roman Catholic church in the province where they lived, probably in the village of Rudamina.

(Years later Verna sent for her baptismal records but they were unavailable. The church had burnt to the ground.)

Living in Lithuania was difficult. Martinas and his brothers farmed small plots of land that did not satisfy their needs. They couldn't raise enough crops or livestock to feed their families adequately, much less sell for cash in the small markets.

Stories that told about jobs with good salaries in America began to cross the border from Prussia. Book smugglers, men who secretly traveled to neighboring countries to purchase books banned by the Russian Czar, met with young men and women and related tales about recruiters who would pay their passage to the New World. Martinas decided to go to America, probably reasoning that after he became a rich man he would send for his wife and children. He approached the only man in the area who could write and asked him to send a request for a ship-card to his friend, Mr. Pajaujis, in the United States of America.

"Don't worry," Martinas probably told Ona. "I'll hide from the Russian soldiers in the forests of birch trees during the day, and walk to Prussia on the open roads only at night." Lithuania was under Russian domination, and the Emperor had decreed that no young man or woman was permitted to leave the country. Martinas surely didn't possess enough rubles to ride the trains, which had recently arrived in Lithuania.

"I'll get rich fast and send for you to come to America to live with me," were his parting words to Ona, as he held back his tears. They were both young and had been married only three years. He feared that they might never see each other again, but he was determined to make this long and burdensome trip.

As he walked from his home he probably turned often to see Ona standing in the doorway holding baby Jonas in her arms. Little Veronika could have been sobbing and waving goodbye, hiding her face in her mother's apron. Ona must have followed Martinas with her eyes until he disappeared from view.

❖

At the border he paid the guide to make an arrangement with the Russian sentry to steal him across. While the guard patrolled the opposite end of his sector, Martinas ran across the border into Prussia. From there he went on to Rotterdam, Holland, where he remained in a room with other travelers until their ship was ready to leave. Before boarding the vessel that would take him to America he was vaccinated and disinfected, and the hair on his head was shaved to rid him of possible lice, which often carried typhus.

He traveled steerage, the lowest and cheapest part of the ship which, we read, was crammed with several hundred men, women, and children. The ventilation was almost nonexistent. The food served aboard ship consisted of lukewarm soup, boiled potatoes, stringy beef or herring, bread, and tea. Many passengers carried their own black bread and slabs of corned meat.

Chapter Six

Huckleberries and Mushrooms

I n his Declaration of Intention for naturalization, No. 907, Martinas Matusevicius stated that in 1901, on or about August 15, the ship in which he traveled to America arrived at the New York port of entry.

We can easily visualize the scene. Twenty-six years of age, he rushed to disembark with the mob of men and women who had traveled with him on this sea voyage of three weeks duration.

To take his first look at his new land he stretched his head up high to see between his fellow travelers, and pushed with all the others who carried large bundles over their shoulders, in their

"HE RUSHED TO DISEMBARK WITH THE MOB OF MEN AND WOMEN . . . ."

Immigrants arriving in New York City

(photo courtesy of Eckley Miners' Village Museum)

arms, and on their backs. According to his Certificate of Naturalization he was only five feet two inches tall.

Butterflies fluttered in his stomach; he had finally reached his destination. Troubled, frightened, and sad when he remembered the family he had left behind, he smiled when he thought of the riches he would acquire in this land of opportunity. Even the many friends he made aboard ship talked about the gold that they had heard lined the streets in America.

The examination of immigrants was long and unpleasant. They sat and slept for two or three days in a special area set aside for them as they waited their turn to appear before the officials screening them for health problems.

They were questioned, examined, and disinfected from parasites they may have picked up aboard ship. Doctors poked instruments into their eyes and ears. Some of the would-be immigrants did not pass the harsh inspection and were returned to their former countries. Warned by earlier immigrants from Lithuania that he should Americanize his name, Martinas printed Martin Matusevicz on the papers he signed to enter his new country.

When Martin set foot on land, most likely he was greeted by recruiters carrying placards and shouting "Work in the mines in Pennsylvania!", "In Chicago you'll get rich in the slaughterhouses!", "Tailors needed in Baltimore!" Some of the recruiters were themselves immigrants from Lithuania.

❖

Martin traveled by train to the depot at Mount Carmel, Pennsylvania, where he met with his friend Pajaujis. *"Labas"* (Greetings), Pajaujis said, *"Kaip sveikata?"* (How's your health?) The Lithuanian words gave Martin a much-needed dose of comfort after his strenuous journey.

The two men walked together up the Merriam Mountain, past the cemetery at the top, and continued down the hill to the patch town of Merriam. The orange-colored blossoms of the mountain laurel were in full bloom. Martin was probably delighted to notice low bushes covered with large clumps of huckleberries. He also realized that, in the fall, many ripe mushrooms would grow in the marshy soil. "Why, it's no different from Lithuania," he must have thought.

"MARTIN TRAVELED BY TRAIN TO THE DEPOT AT MOUNT CARMEL . . . ."

The railroad station, which was on Market Street, has been demolished

Merriam, a patch town, was built for the miners by the owners of the mines. The houses were close to the colliery and each had two rooms, a large kitchen downstairs and a garret, or attic, upstairs where everyone slept. Thin pieces of wood nailed over the outside seams of the buildings did little to keep out the rain and the cold. On the inside, walls were not plastered—women pasted newspapers and pictures on them for insulation. An outhouse, used by two or three families, stood in the back yard. The coal company deducted from the pay of the miner the high rent they charged for housing.

My mother told me that when her father, Martinas, arrived in Merriam, he moved in with a Lithuanian family, to which he paid a small sum for his daily board. The house was a stone's throw away from the Summit Coal Co. mine, where he went to work immediately.

Martinas, now called Martin, started to work as a "buddy" to an experienced miner from whom he learned the craft of min-

"THE MINER DRILLED HOLES . . . [AND] TAMPED IN THE EXPLOSIVES."
A miner at work
(photo courtesy Eckley Miners' Village Museum)

"THE "BUDDY" SHOVELED . . . CHUNKS OF FALLEN COAL INTO THE MINE CARS."
Mules pull the cars filled with coal
(photo courtesy Eckley Miner's Village Museum)

ing. Each miner began his work as a "buddy", an apprentice to a seasoned miner. The "buddy" brought the miner his tools and supplies, filled his lamp with oil, and did odd jobs. Then the "buddy" watched as the miner drilled holes into the coal seams, tamped in the explosives, and fired them from a safe distance. After the smoke had cleared, the "buddy" shoveled the chunks of fallen coal into the mine cars.

Chapter Seven

Maple Street

In two years Martinas saved enough money to send for his wife, Ona, and his two children, Veronika, my mother, and Jonas, my mother's brother.

My cousin Vince Kaminski (grandson of Ona's sister Rosie) informed me that his and my grandmothers arrived in 1903 in Baltimore, Maryland. I surmise that they traveled by train from there to the depot at Mount Carmel, Pennsylvania, where Martin met them. (There was a train station on Market Street at that time. It no longer exists.)

I am certain that Martinas didn't notice how disheveled Ona and the children looked. They had not bathed in three weeks. Their clothes were wrinkled and smelled of perspiration. Veronika's face had smudges of dirt that Ona tried unsuccessfully to remove. Jonas had remnants of food on his clothing. The children possibly hung close to their mother, afraid to touch this man who was a stranger to them. But Martinas's heart was truly filled with joy. His life would now be complete.

Ona moved into the home Martin had prepared for her, and she made friends with the other Lithuanian immigrant miners' wives and their families. Her best friend was her sister who had traveled together with her from the old country on the same ship. Her sister's name was Rosie, but we the grandchildren always knew her as "Ciuty." (The word for grandmother in Lithuanian is *mociute*. Ciuty is a derivative). Ciuty's husband, Antanas Salasevicius, had sent Ciuty the ship-card. Ciuty's children, Ona (Annie) and Anele (Nellie), traveled with her.

❖

Martinas's wife, Ona, saw that in America life would be different in some ways but remarkably familiar in others. There would not be livestock to tend or fields to harvest, but there would

"CIUTY'S CHILDREN . . . [HAD] TRAVELED WITH HER."
*"Ciuty" Salaseviciene (Ona Matuseviciene's sister, Rose) and her daughter Nellie
sit on the steps of the house on Spruce Street, c. 1939*

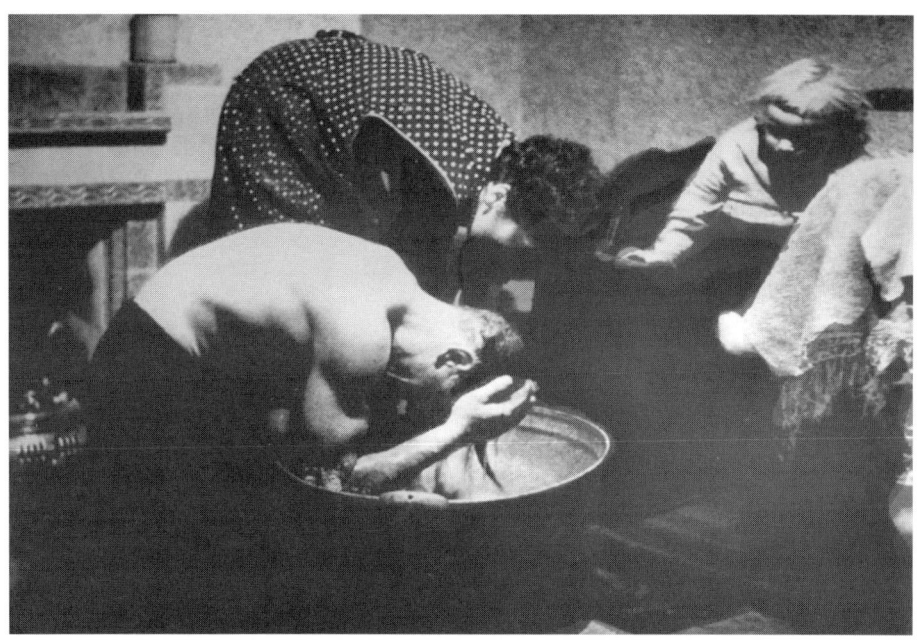

"SHE BOILED WATER AND CARRIED IT TO THE WASHTUB..."
Bathing after a day's work in the mines
(photo courtesy Eckley Miners' Village Museum)

still be a garden to weed, housework to do, meals to prepare, parties and dances to go to, and a church to attend.

It was nice living near the homes of other people. In Lithuania the houses on the farms were far apart, sometimes miles. Ona's new friends taught her how to cope with the responsibilities of a housewife. In a short time her days became routine.

At the end of each day she boiled water and carried it to the washtub in the kitchen, where she scrubbed the coal soot from her husband's back as he sat and bathed himself. Mondays, she washed clothes by hand and hung them outside on lines to dry, even in the dead of winter on icy cold days. Tuesdays, she ironed clothes, heating the iron on the back burner of the stove. Wednesdays, she sewed and darned torn clothing.

Thursdays, she baked enough bread to last the whole week. Fridays, she cleaned the house, swept the coal dust from the floors, and hung every pillow, blanket, and feather tick (comforter) out the window to air. All the windows in the house were washed.

Saturdays, she waited in long lines to draw water from the pump down the street. She boiled and poured the water into the wooden tubs in the kitchen so that she and her children could bathe.

❖

Sundays, Ona (now known as Annie), Martin, and their children—Veronika (Verna) and Jonas (John)—walked to church and enjoyed conversation with friends. Annie also learned how to brew beer and make *boilo*, the Lithuanian whiskey boiled with herbs. Making *boilo* was possible only when Annie could obtain all the necessary ingredients: caraway seeds, cinnamon, nutmeg, ginger, cloves, honey, oranges, lemons, and a fifth of rye.

According to the 1910 census Martin and Annie rented a home at 332 South Maple Street in Mount Carmel, and the 1920 census showed them living a few doors down, at 312 South Maple Street. Martin's trade was mining, and he worked close by in the Reliance Colliery. Two more boys had been born to the family—Joseph in 1904, and Stanley in 1908. A third boy, George, was born in 1906, but his name was not entered into the 1910 census. My guess is that George's omission from the 1910 census was an oversight. George lived a long life. I knew him well. (His name did appear in the 1920 census.)

Annie liked living on Maple Street because she could walk to the Holy Cross Lithuanian Church for daily Mass. Verna and John could attend school close by. Annie helped to support the family by taking in boarders. The 1910 census mentions that three Lithuanian immigrants, Joe Malinowski, Joe Bulcavitch, and Anthony Pavis, lived with them. (This is not the same Pavis who sent the ship-card.)

The homes on Maple Street were attached houses built on a little hill. At the top of the street was a set of train tracks on which trains roared through the town two or three times a day. Although children were ordered not to play near the tracks, they liked to wave to people sitting in the cars as the trains sped past.

On the afternoon of July 28, 1909, Annie heard the train come to a screeching halt. Frightened, she ran with her neighbors to the corner to discover a young child lying on the tracks under the train.

"Martin and Annie rented a home at 332 Maple Street . . . ."
Martin and Annie made wine from the grapes they grew behind the house, c. 1910

"JOHNNY JOINED THE YOUNG BOYS WHO WORKED AT THE 'BREAKER' . . . ."
Reliance Breaker; most of the workers were children because the men were needed in the mines

Joseph, only five years old, had been killed instantly. Neighbors rallied around her as with uncontrollable sobs she screamed to her son, "Wake up! Why did you disobey me? You were my first American son. Don't leave me!"

Years later she talked about her son Joseph, but with a cold detached feeling. She had shed many sad tears and thought of him often, but life had to go on. She suppressed her sorrow and turned her mind to taking care of her remaining offspring. Early death for children from illness or accident was not unexpected in those days.

Through the years life became a little easier for Annie as the family's income grew. Martin was promoted to coal-miner status. Their daughter Verna left school after the third grade and worked at the cigar factory rolling tobacco leaves into cigars. Johnny joined the young boys who worked at the "breaker," picking out and discarding the rock, slate, and other refuse that came down the chutes with the coal. (The breaker was a large structure at the mouth of a coal mine, where coal brought up from the mine would be broken, cleaned, sized, and sorted for market.)

Chapter Eight

A New Citizen

January 18, 1915, was a memorable day: Martin realized his dream to become an American citizen. His Certificate of Naturalization (a copy of which we requested and received from the Northumberland County Prothonotary in Sunbury, Pennsylvania), described him as thirty-nine years old, five feet two inches tall, white color, light complexion, brown eyes and brown hair. He had visible distinguishing marks of smallpox on his face and resided at 312 South Maple Street in Mount Carmel, Pennsylvania.

The certificate stated that his wife, Annie, was thirty-five. There were five children: Veronica, born March 15, 1899; John, born August 14, 1901; George, born April 16, 1906; Stanley, born December 1, 1908; and Charles, born March 3, 1912. Martin stated that he was formerly a subject of Nicholas, Emperor of all the Russias. Instead of writing in cursive he printed his name as Martin Matusevicz on the signature line. (Perhaps this means that he could only print.)

A short time later, Verna, 15 years of age, came home from work and announced, "I'm getting married. I'm marrying Wally Shierant."

Annie and Martin were aghast. "You're too young. You can't do that, and besides, he's Polish, not Lithuanian."

"I don't care, he's the guy I want to marry and you can't stop me."

Annie was in tears. "What'll I say to my friends? How will I face them? There are so many nice Lithuanian boys."

"Mom, I don't want a Lithuanian boy, I want Wally!"

"Stasys is nice. He's strong, works hard. He'll bring home a lot of money to take care of you."

"Pop, I don't want Stasys. You can have him. I'm marrying Wally Shierant."

"HIS WIFE, ANNIE, WAS THIRTY-FIVE. THERE WERE FIVE CHILDREN . . . ."
Stanley, John, George, c. 1939 (Verna and Charles were absent; a sixth child, Joe, had been killed earlier)

Verna married Wally on May 30, 1916. They lived with Verna's mother and dad for a short time but later settled about three miles away from Mount Carmel, in Kulpmont, where they began to raise their own family. Annie and Martin were devastated. Their firstborn had left their nest. She lived too far away. They could not visit daily. To visit her only daughter Annie rode the trolley cars from Oak Street in Mount Carmel to Kulpmont. Occasionally, if she felt well, and the weather was comfortable, she walked the distance.

"ANNIE RODE THE TROLLEY CARS FROM OAK STREET . . . TO KULPMONT."

A view to the north on Oak Street, c. 1919

Martin began to suffer more and more from miner's asthma, the illness he contracted from breathing dust-laden air in the depths of the mines. His last days were spent in much distress. The illness had robbed his lungs of breathing power, and one could hear him struggling with moments of spasmodic gasping for air. Annie, frightened, would listen and run to him with a little glass of schnapps, hoping it would give him some relief. In those days there was little medication to help. The disease finally claimed his life on May 12, 1924.

He lay in an open casket in the parlor of his home, where neighbors and friends came for three days and nights to extend their sympathies to Annie and her children. Martin was buried on the top of Merriam Mountain in Holy Cross cemetery.

After the funeral, friends and relatives came back to the house and feasted on fresh *kielbasa* (homemade sausage), rye bread, homemade beer, and *boilo*.

❖

Annie continued to live at 312 South Maple Street. At first her sons stayed with her, but in a few years Stanley (called Tiny) moved to New Britain, Connecticut, to work in a factory making locks. He came home only for visits. But when he retired from his work, he came back to live his last days in Mount Carmel. Annie's son George danced his way through life, never had a serious job, and died an alcoholic.

John (Johnny) the oldest son, married Anna Kersavage, a nurse who lived in Mahanoy City, Pennsylvania. This surprised and irritated his mother since she expected Johnny to wed Emma Petchulis, a teacher who lived in Mount Carmel and with whom she was very well acquainted. She felt that Mahanoy City was too far away, and Anna Kersavage was a stranger to her. But Anna helped Annie through many an illness, and they became friends.

Charles (Charlie), the youngest son, went to Pittston, Pennsylvania, to work in the mines. There he met and married Elizabeth Pavlico.

Annie was always a foreigner in the United States. She was a heavy woman and seemed to wonder what to do in her new world. She never learned to read, write, or speak English,

"At first her sons stayed with her . . . ."
Annie Matuseviciene with her youngest son, Charles, c. 1934

always made meals in one large pot, and served them on the table in one big bowl. She had very few friends. Her best friend was still Ciuty, her sister Rose, who came to America at the same time that she did.

Ciuty, who also never learned English, had moved with her husband to Spruce Street in Mount Carmel and came to visit her often.

Annie's life centered around her children and their children. I'll never forget that brick she warmed all day on the back of the coal stove and placed at my feet when we slept together in the attic. The only heat in the house was in the kitchen two flights down, but we were warm under a fluffy, full feather tick that she had made herself with goose feathers.

Sometime in 1929 my parents moved to 239 West Fifth Street in Mount Carmel. Annie walked daily the three short blocks from her home on Maple Street to our home. She liked to sit on the front porch and converse with the people strolling up and down the sidewalk.

Often gran'mam (our name for Annie) and I would walk up Merriam hill towards the cemetery. We'd pass mountain laurel bushes in bloom with colorful pink and orange blossoms, and we'd search for huckleberry bushes. When she'd find a bush filled with clumps of huckleberries, she'd point to it and say, "Leona, sit here in the middle of the bush and pick!" I had difficulty understanding her Lithuanian (I never learned to speak it well), but I knew what she meant. I'd find an open spot, sit down in it, and start picking the huckleberries to put into the can strapped with twine around my neck.

In the meantime she would fill cans that were three or four times the size of mine. We liked picking huckleberries. They were on very low bushes so that we'd have to stoop or sit in the midst of the dense branches to reach the huckleberries. I'll always remember their juicy sweet taste when I ate a few as I picked the dark blue succulent berries that I found in the bushes.

When we brought the berries home Annie would wash and clean them well so that they could be baked into pies. My mother, Verna, would pile the berries high in her handmade pie crusts and add a little sugar. To this day I have not tasted pies as delicious as those made from the huckleberries we picked on Merriam Mountain and baked in the hot oven of the kitchen stove fired by coal.

In the fall we would look through damp ground for mushrooms. Annie also knew how to differentiate between good and bad mushrooms. She especially enjoyed picking mushrooms. I felt that it brought back to her many memories of the old country.

On July 4, 1941, Annie, never a very healthy person, suffered a heart attack in the middle of the night. Anna, John's wife, phoned to my mother Verna and alerted her to come quickly. Annie was very ill, and might be dying. Verna rushed to Annie's side to discover that she was breathing with intense effort. Annie was slowly giving up her life.

Both Verna and Anna were with Annie when she passed away. Verna later related this story that my sister, Irene, recalls: "One solitary tear dropped from her eyes, and she passed away quietly before a doctor could reach her."

Martinas and Ona never returned to Lithuania to see again their parents, their homestead, their siblings, or their friends. Neither one of them ever attended school. Their immediate children had little education, only learned to read and write.

But, as Martin and Annie, they started a dynasty in America. Today their grandchildren and great grandchildren live in six different states of the United States. They have traveled to different parts of the world. Many have earned college degrees. Some of them have even been to Lithuania, which Martin and Annie saw only in their dreams after they had migrated from their homeland to America, their land of opportunity.

Book Three

Juozas and Ona Guzevicius

LITHUANIA 1992

It rains every day. Our feet
Swim in puddles of water.
The wind pounds, smashes
Us for venturing out to attack it.
We dress to battle nature,
Wrap our shivering bodies with
Two sweaters, a jacket, heavy wool mittens,
A sturdy cap, an overlarge scarf.

We walk the streets.
Cars are old. There are no cars.
Petrol is expensive. There is no petrol.
Buses carry the world in their bellies,
Limp along forming arcs with their bottoms
From the weight of their fullness.
No vacancies for new travelers.

On the esplanade by the marketplace
Half a world away from where I live
Stalin's face lies shattered over the earth

LS/G

Chapter Nine

Juozas in Lithuania

It was a sunny but cool and comfortable day in October, one of the days New England is proud to own, and we were visiting Juozas (Joe) and Ona Guzevicius, my husband's parents. When we arrived, they were searching through old periodicals and mail they had received many years earlier.

As he reopened a much faded envelope, Joe explained that the letter had arrived in early 1924. The message was from Anele, his youngest sister, whom he had never seen because she entered the world after he had left the family farm in the village of Zovoda, Lithuania.

His shoulders drooped and his eyes filled with tears when he read once again the much wrinkled printed note. "My mother

"'My mother died . . . . This photo shows her body in a casket.'"
Marija, Jule, Anele, sisters of Juozas Guzevicius, c. 1923

died November 27, 1923. This photo shows her body in a casket. The people standing are my sisters."

A few hours later Joe began to tell us his story. "My father, Vincas, was a tyrant who beat his wife and children. According to Lithuanian standards he was a wealthy man, the unofficial mayor and banker of Zovoda, a village approximately eight kilometers north of Punskas, where all the children were baptized in the Catholic church. He was also the owner of sixty *markes* of land (approximately seventy-five acres), a vast area for a farmer in the old country. Farmers came to his home to borrow money, and when their widows couldn't repay the loans, his farm grew larger. His house teemed with children, and his many servants were unwanted maiden aunts and destitute cousins.

"Somewhere he had learned to inject into a healthy leg a serum that would cause a permanent limp. Young men from the village came to him for the injections, so that they would not have to spend years of involuntary service in the Imperial Russian Army. Papa was also skilled in treating horses' ailments. He had the ability to discern the illness of the animal, and administer with compassion suitable medicines.

"His attitude at home to his children was different. I hated him because he drank too much and displayed uncontrollable anger at the slightest provocation.

"My mama, Josefina Zuikaite, was also known as Juzefa Zuikyte before she wed my papa. She was a hardworking woman but after her marriage suffered many insults and angry outbursts from my papa. Mama had eighteen children with papa, ten of whom survived: Jonas, Stasys, Antanas, Pranas, Vladas, Marija, Vincas, Jule, Anele, and I, Juozas. Jonas and Antanas emigrated to Canada soon after I left to sail for America. My other siblings remained in Lithuania."

My father-in-law, Juozas, continued to tell us how unhappy he was in the old country. He had always loved books and wanted to be a doctor, but after he had one year of schooling, his father decided he was old enough to work on the farm. Although he and his brothers spent long hours digging, seeding, planting, and reaping the land, there was never enough to eat.

❖

"Meat was available only for my father at the dinner table," said Juozas, continuing the story of his life as a child in his father's house. "We, his children, were permitted one small bite of pork or chicken about once a week. A large pot, filled with vegetables from our farm, sat in the center of the table during our meal. We'd dip our bowls into the stew and look to see if papa was watching. Then we'd try to get one of the rare pieces of meat that mama put in for taste. If papa caught us he would lean over and forcibly beat our knuckles with the back of the spoon. Our papa was strong and I can still feel the pain he inflicted. I had difficulty using my hands for many days.

"I remember that in the winter mama made hot meals from vegetables she preserved during the summer and fall. She preserved cucumbers in brine and made sauerkraut by cutting cabbage very fine and, adding salt, fermenting it in its own juice in a round wooden barrel about six feet high. The apples, pears, and cherries that grew in papa's orchard had to be preserved in jars for future consumption. Mama also baked her own bread.

"Papa planted and harvested rye, wheat, barley, oats, potatoes, beets, and carrots. His livestock consisted of cows, sheep, geese, ducks, chickens, and horses. We worked from early morning until late night since we also prepared the food to feed the animals. We gathered the grain in large wagons and transported it to the markets to be sold to friends, neighbors, and others."

Juozas was nearing the age of conscription into the Russian army, certain death because those of Lithuanian descent were put into the front lines. He began to hear many stories about the riches of that faraway land America, and saw advertisements offering jobs with good wages. Friends and relatives who had traveled to the new country were sending money and gifts home to their families. Letters arrived describing work for everyone, wages paid for labor, and ability to purchase food and clothing. Surely, he reasoned, the streets in America were paved with gold.

When he told his father that he wanted to go to America, his father was dismayed and tried to dissuade him from leaving the homeland.

"You are a good farmer. You love the land and have a natural ability to make crops grow. If you stay I may give you land of your own to prepare and cultivate. You'll do very well working at something you love and understand."

Juozas, however, was determined to travel to America. He wrote to a boyhood friend who had gone there earlier, and requested his friend to purchase a ship-card for him. He would reimburse him the thirty dollars when he reached America and got a job. He waited a long time for a reply and feared his mail was lost, but he finally received a letter with the much desired ship-card.

"Mama cried when I told her I was going to America, but she did not stop me. I walked to the top of the hill and turned around to take a last look at my home. That masonry cottage with a straw thatched roof sheltered by many tall birch trees and a few apple trees will always remain in my memory. I saw the white wooden picket fence in front of the house and looked at the hens trotting up and down the pathway. I felt I was deserting my family and my life, but I was determined to continue on to America. My mama was standing in the doorway waving to me. I saw her pick up the bottom of her apron to wipe her eyes and knew she was weeping. I never saw her again."

❖

Juozas walked to Prussia from his home. Since he possessed a limited amount of Russian rubles he could not ride the trains, which had recently arrived in Lithuania.

At the border Juozas asked the guide to approach the Russian sentry with a bribe to look away as Juozas crossed over to Prussia. From Prussia Juozas found his way to Hamburg, Germany. There he paid a small fee to stay in a room with other potential travelers until the ship was ready to sail. Before embarking he was vaccinated and disinfected, and his head was shaved to reduce the risk of lice and the typhus they might carry.

Recently we obtained a copy of his Petition of Naturalization, Number 66562, from Washington, D.C. It was dated October 26, 1921, and indicated that Juozas was born August 25, 1892. We also discovered from this document that the *Bluecher*, the ship that would take him to America, set sail from Hamburg, Germany, on or about June 7, 1913.

At the University of Baltimore, in the Steamship Historical Society of America Collection at the Langsdale Library, we found

"... THE *BLUECHER*, THE SHIP THAT WOULD TAKE [JUOZAS] TO AMERICA ...."

His voyage was from Hamburg, Germany, to East Boston, Massachusetts

the book *Passenger Ships of the World, Past and Present,* which describes the ship *Bluecher*. The *Bluecher* was built in 1901 by Blohm & Voss in Hamburg, Germany. Tonnage 12,334; dimensions 525' x 62' at the waterline, 550' overall length; twin screw; 16½ knots; quadruple-expansion engine; 2 masts; 2 funnels. Passengers: 390 first-class; 230 second; and 550 third (steerage).*

We surmise that Juozas traveled third-class with several hundred other passengers who were looking forward to finding a better life in America. Juozas mentioned to us that many travelers carried black bread, to relieve the hunger they felt from the meager food they received on board ship.

*Eugene W. Smith, *Passenger Ships of the World, Past and Present,* 2nd ed. (Boston: G.H. Dean, 1978), p. 32.

Chapter Ten

Juozas Arrives in America

On June 19, 1913, the *Bluecher* arrived in East Boston, Massachusetts. Standing steady in the front of the mob pressing forward to disembark, Juozas, twenty-one years of age, must have gazed at the sight before him. He had finally reached his destination. Tears surely came to his eyes as he thought of his homeland, his mother, and his siblings back in Lithuania at the farm. But he probably smiled when he remembered that he did not have to face the cruelty of his father or conscription into the Russian army. In his mind he could see freedom and his right to choose how he would live the remainder of his life. This is America, he would have thought, the land of opportunity. He must work diligently and make a good life for the family he hoped to have.

Juozas, along with all the other immigrants who wished to enter the new land, stayed in an area set aside for them for about two or three days until they were summoned for a physical examination. Juozas was concerned whether he would pass the rigid test to enter this wonderful country, America. He heard from earlier immigrants who had endured the examination that the testing was long and painful.

He expected to be fumigated for parasites since Americans were worried about dangerous insects entering the country. This, he thought, was wise. But Juozas also had heard that some earlier immigrants failed the inspection and were compelled to go back to their former country. "I am strong and healthy," he said to himself, "I will surely be accepted in my new country."

Juozas approached the immigration officials with some apprehension. He had been told that he would have difficulty getting work with his Lithuanian name. Somehow he must let the officials who would examine his traveling certificates know that he wanted to change his name. He hoped that they would be happy to know that he wished to become an American even before he touched the soil of his new land.

To his surprise the young man standing beside the welcoming official spoke Lithuanian. "Where did you come from?" Juozas asked. "Did you come from Punskas, my part of the country?"

"No, I was born in the north, and I have been here ten years. I welcome you and hope you'll be happy in America also."

"I want to change my name to Joseph Guzievyc. Is this possible?" "Yes, it is. We'll change it on your passport now. *Sekmes Amerike!*" (Good Luck in America!)

Juozas, now to be known as Joseph, with the help of sympathetic interpreters purchased railroad tickets to Worcester, Massachusetts. Only ten cents remained in his pocket, and he was looking forward to the help he would receive from the friend who had sent him the ship-card. This friend would be waiting for him in Worcester.

But when he arrived at his destination no one was there to greet him. He continued walking along strange streets until suddenly he heard familiar words. A group of people assembled on the sidewalk and steps in front of a nearby building were speaking Lithuanian. He was excited when he stopped to greet them and asked if they knew his friend who had sent him the ship-card. None of the group recognized the name of his sponsor. Realizing his predicament, his new acquaintances took him to the Lithuanian Club where he could stay until he found the friend who had sent him the ship-card.

After many days of fruitless searching Joseph concluded that his friend had forgotten him, and he approached his newfound allies for advice. They told him about a farmer in Charlton, Massachusetts, who was looking for a strong man to work on his land. Yankees hired immigrants because their labor was cheap.

The owner of the farm liked Joseph, now known as Joe, because Joseph knew how to fertilize the land with cow manure. His carrots, potatoes, cabbage, beets, and turnips grew large and healthy looking.

Another farmhand worked with Joe, and every day they had cows to milk. Joe always finished in half the time. His co-worker was beside himself to know his secret, but Joe never told him that he took the cows' teats between the fingers of his strong hands four at a time (two with each hand) and quickly drained the cow dry.

Joe worked every day for six months before he was given some free time. He put the few dollars he had earned into his pocket and, wearing the same outfit he wore when he left Lithuania, Joe traveled by train to Worcester, to the large department store nicknamed the "beautiful palace store" by the immigrants. Joe purchased pants, shoes, a shirt, and a sweater.

Attired in his new American clothes he visited his friends at the Lithuanian Club. They were astonished that, in such a short time in America, he had acquired enough English vocabulary to do his own purchasing. Not many were familiar with enough of the language that they could venture out alone as he had.

After two or three years working on the farm, during which he traveled to town as often as he could to visit his Lithuanian friends, Joe eventually decided to leave the farm and move to town. He wished to stay near others of Lithuanian descent, so he found a job in a factory, a wire mill, where he became a semiskilled machine operator.

We are not certain how Joe encountered his wife, Ona, in America, since he lived in Worcester, Massachusetts, and she lived forty miles away in South Boston. In conversations with Lithuanian immigrants we learned that the Lithuanians often assembled in groups and had many parties and other social gatherings. It is very possible they met in the following fashion:

> One day Joe and his friends learned that the Lithuanian community in South Boston was planning a festivity in honor of St. Casimir, the patron saint of their home country. They made arrangements to travel by train to South Boston. There they found countrymen celebrating with parades, parties, and meetings with old friends.
>
> At a party, Joe was dancing the polka with the wife of one of his Worcester friends when he noticed a group of young women dancing with each other, circling the room with such energy and grace that everyone stopped to look. One woman

"YOU LOOK DIFFERENT IN AN AMERICAN DRESS."
Ona Kubiliute, c. 1914

especially caught his attention. She wore a white dress nipped in at a tiny waistline and long enough to touch her ankles.

As she stepped lightly to the polka rhythms, her skirt twirled revealing kidskin pointed toe oxfords. Lisle hose covered her firm shapely legs. A ribbon with sprigs of ruta (rue) circled her head, adorning the long curly locks that fell to her shoulders. Her exuberant dancing brought a rosy color to her cheeks, and there was a strange, familiar look about her.

I must meet her, Joe thought. At the intermission he walked slowly to where she was standing. "Gera diena" (Good day), he said, "I like the way you dance. Will you polka with me?"

"Juozas," she said, using his Lithuanian name, "When did you come to America? Don't you remember me? I'm Ona Kubiliute."

Joe was surprised and embarrassed. "You look different in an American dress. I did not recognize you. You are very pretty!"

Chapter Eleven

Ona's Journey

O na and Juozas had been neighbors in Lithuania. The farm-house where Ona lived was on a low hill within walking distance to Juozas' homestead. As children they had climbed trees, picked apples, and walked through moist lands looking for mushrooms together.

We think that Ona Kubiliute had arrived in America a few months before Juozas, but we know that she had not experienced the same difficulties Juozas had to endure. Her sister Magdalena, the oldest sibling, came to America first and was already married to a young Lithuanian lad Jurgis (George) Valatka. Magdalena was pregnant with her first child when she sent a letter to Ona.

"Come to America and live with me. It's a wonderful country. There is enough work for many people, and we are paid good wages. There are also young handsome Lithuanian men looking for wives. You are strong and pretty, you will get a good husband," Magdalena wrote to her sister. "I will buy a ship-card and send it to you."

Ona was intrigued with the news she had heard from her sister. Her mother Katrina (Kalinauskaite) Kubiliene and her other siblings—Jokubas, Katrina, Augustas, Vincas, and Pranas—urged her to take advantage of this opportunity.

The story of Magdalena Kubiliute's coming to America was explained to my husband Albert by his cousin Viktor Kubilius, whose father was Jokubas, the brother of Albert's aunt Magdalena and mother Ona.

Magdalena had arrived in America in 1910 after receiving a ship-card from her brother Jokubas in 1909. "Men of marriageable age are scarce in Lithuania," he wrote. "They have either emigrated to America or they have perished in the ravages of battle in the Russian Czar's forces. You will find someone quickly to marry in America."

Jokubas had emigrated to the United States in 1906 in order to evade the threat of conscription into the Czar's Russian Army. In America he met his future wife, Katrina Budzeikaite, a Lithuanian girl who lived in South Boston. They were wed in St. Peter's Lithuanian Church on February 26, 1911.

In 1910, Liudvikas, the father of the Kubilius family, passed away in Lithuania. Magdalena, the oldest sibling still living at the family home, became the caretaker of her siblings. She desperately wanted to take advantage of the ship-card that her brother Jokubas had sent her the year before, and travel to America.

Magdalena departed from the homestead in Lithuania and traveled to America. Ona, the next sibling in line, became the official caretaker. Magdalena probably promised Ona that she would send a ship-card to her at the earliest opportunity.

❖

When Magdalena arrived in America her name was changed to "Margaret." Her first duties were to look after the boarders in Jokubas's home and carry out all the functions of housework. Soon however, she sought and found a position in a men's clothing factory, where she became a tailor.

In 1911, Magdalena (now known as Margaret) met Jurgis (George) Valatka, another young Lithuanian immigrant. They married on November 17, 1912, and immediately rented their own apartment in South Boston.

❖

Elinor Marcel, Margaret's first child, described the building in which Margaret, George, and their children lived. "The house, a three stories high newly built structure, was on Gold Street in South Boston. A different family lived on each floor, and each family had boarders, newly arrived Lithuanian immigrants. The house contained an interesting, very distinctive element. In place of an outhouse, a single privy, connected to the city sewer, dominated the basement and was used with delight by all the tenants of the building. Everyone also took advantage of a Turkish bathhouse nearby for a weekly body cleansing."

❖

Viktor Kubilius related that after the death of Liudvikas, father of the Kubilius family, Viktor's father Jokubas realized that as the eldest son he had a claim to the homestead in Lithuania. Although his wife, Katrina, was pregnant he decided to return to the "old country." Since he was married he was no longer subject to conscription in the Russian Czar's army. Jokubas and Katrina departed from America in 1911 and, soon after their arrival in their home country, a daughter, Ona, entered the world. (As of this year, 2002, Ona, daughter of Jokubas and Katrina, is 91 years old and still lives in Lithuania. Ona was never wed.)

When Magdalena was settled in her new home she sent the promised ship-card to Ona, her sister and my mother-in-law. When Ona Kubiliute, the future mother of my husband Albert, received the ship-card from her sister Magdalena (Margaret), she had an intense desire to emigrate to America. Katrina, who had returned to Lithuania from America with her husband Jokubas, now became the caretaker of the family that remained in Lithuania.

❖

In one of her reminiscences, Ona Kubiliute Guzeviciene told Albert, her son and my husband, the story of her trip to America, which he related to me.

Ona packed her possessions carefully into a large hand-woven linen shawl, wore three petticoats and two jackets to save baggage, sewed her remaining rubles into a belt around her waist, and walked to the border. But she was not alone. Ona joined a group of young men and women who were also taking this arduous journey.

They had been warned by imperial authorities not to leave their country, or they would be detained and prosecuted, so they walked through the fields at night and hid deep in the forests during the day to evade officers searching for possible travelers.

At the border Ona paid the guide the necessary fee to steal her across when the Russian sentry was patrolling another area. She bought a train ticket to Antwerp, Belgium, the port of embarkation for America. In Antwerp Ona and a group of girls from other parts of Lithuania rented a room together as they waited for the ship on which they would sail to their new country.

❖

In later years, Ona also related to her son Albert how she enjoyed walking the streets in Antwerp, viewing strange city buildings, and sitting in parks. She and her new friends were fascinated with the trolleys and could not resist the temptation to see where the cars were going.

Giggling as they pulled up their skirts to climb the few steps into the car, they shook their shoulders and smiled at the conductor who held his hand out to them and spoke a language they didn't understand. They sat down comfortably on the seats and wondered why the man was so agitated.

They spent a pleasant afternoon, called each other's attention to the different kinds of architecture, and continued to smile at the frenzied conductor. Suddenly they became alarmed because they didn't recognize the buildings and streets they were passing. They remained on the cars praying 'Hail Marys' under their breath, and to their relief, familiar houses began to reappear. They were happy to leave the trolley and the man who talked too much to them. Much later they discovered that they should have paid for the trip with Belgian francs, which they did not possess.

Ona Kubiliute and her friends were also vaccinated and disinfected, and their hair brushed and searched for lice, before they were permitted to board the ship. They traveled steerage for ten days, and in March, 1913, reached the port of entry at East Boston, Massachusetts. Ona Kubiliute was twenty-four years of age.

Magdalena (Margaret) met Ona when she arrived, helped her go through the intricacies of entering the country, and took her to her home, the flat on Gold Street in South Boston where she lived with her husband George.

Ona knew she had to begin working immediately, and her sister Margaret discovered a position for her in which she sewed men's and women's suits for a tailor whose workplace was close enough to walk.

Ona loved her new country and the graceful, dignified styles that American women wore. She was soon visiting the large department store to buy American shoes, hats, and lace-trimmed women's union suits.

Ona confessed to me that she sewed most of her outfits. She

"MAGDALENA (MARGARET) MET ONA WHEN SHE ARRIVED . . . ."
Margaret Valatkiene and Ona Kubiliute, c. 1914

"SHE IS ATTIRED IN AMERICAN FASHIONS OF THE ERA."
Ona Kubiliute, c. 1915

searched for patterns to make herself skirts, blouses, dresses, and a coat in the fashion prevalent among American women at that time. This was evident to us when we viewed her photographs. She is attired in American fashions of the era. According to *The American Mail Order Fashions,** the kidskin pointed toe, fox-heel oxfords were popular footwear. To purchase these fashionable shoes she probably had to go without lunch for a week to save up the $1.25 cost of the pointed toe footwear.

Ona was surely excited when she heard about the Lithuanian celebration in honor of St. Casimir. It is possible that she remarked to her sister Margaret, "I'll sew a new dress. I'm glad I bought the kidskin pointed toe oxfords. They'll look nice when I twirl around as I dance the polkas. I'll fix my long hair in tiny ringlets that'll fall to my shoulders."

"You'll look American, not Lithuanian, and the men from our country will laugh at you," Ona's sister Margaret replied. "You need a husband. Don't spoil your chances to get a man. Lithuanian men marry women who look Lithuanian."

Ona was disturbed at first, but she made a lovely long white dress in fabric with embossed designs, with a high lace collar and 3/4-length sleeves. The dress was nipped in at her slender waist. She also stepped into the kidskin, pointed toe, fox-heel oxfords.

*American Mail Order Fashions 1880-1900 (Scotia, NY: Americana Review, c. 1961), p. 28.

Chapter Twelve

Ona Marries Juozas

"I was happy when I saw Ona," Joe said as he continued his story. "I always liked to talk with her in Lithuania. She was a strong person and gave me some good ideas about how to plant potatoes and beets. When I met her in America I thought she would be a good wife. But I was a little timid because she looked pretty in her white dress with the *ruta* in her hair. I saw her trim and dainty ankles when she twirled during the polka, and I wanted to squeeze her tight and make her my own."

Years later Ona communicated the following events to me, her daughter-in-law Leona. Juozas (Joe) traveled to South Boston on Sundays and holidays in order to see Ona. They'd visit with friends at the Lithuanian Club, where sausage, rye bread, cabbage, beet soup, and the Lithuanian specialty *boilo* were served.

Joe visited Ona many times before he asked her to marry him. According to Lithuanian custom he had to get permission for marriage from her parents first, but they lived far away in a country across the Atlantic Ocean, so he made the request to Ona's sister Margaret, who immediately replied, "Yes."

But Ona wasn't very pleased when Joe asked her to become his wife. "I don't have a nice trousseau," she said. "You must give me time to collect some things."

"That doesn't bother me. We can buy anything we need after we are married," he told her.

"Oh no," she said, "I would be ashamed. I can't marry without a suitable collection of embroidered sheets, towels, and other hand made items a new bride needs."

Actually Ona did not want to get married but she didn't know how to tell Joe. When she explained to her sister that she could not marry him, Margaret was angry. "You will marry him.

You can't afford not to marry him. You are too old to meet another man. You are already twenty-four years old."

"But, Magdyte (Ona's affectionate name for her sister Margaret), I'm not sure I love him."

"Love doesn't matter. You need a man and Joe wants to marry you. He will give you a good home."

"But, sister, I'll have to move to Worcester. I'll be far away from you and my Lithuanian friends in South Boston," Ona begged.

"If you don't marry him you'll never get married. You can't live with me anymore. You must take Joe as your husband because you'll never meet another man as good as he is."

As a matter of fact, it seems that my mother-in-law Ona confided the tale about her desire to reject Joe's marriage proposal and her sister Margaret's reaction only to me and to nobody else. After she was married, she never mentioned dissatisfaction in her life with Joe to her sister, her children, or her friends. Her marriage to Joe always appeared happy and normal. I don't know why Ona made these remarks only to me and never to anyone else.

❖

Ona always seemed content and pleased with her husband and her new home. I still remember the delicious apple pies she enjoyed baking for Joe and her children weekly. Joe would consume an entire pie at one time. As a result, my father-in-law became overweight. Later in his life, Joe became concerned about his obesity, and he managed to lose a considerable amount of heaviness.

Ona married Joe in South Boston at St. Peter's Lithuanian Church on February 14, 1916. The hem of the simple white silk dress she wore stopped at her ankles so that matching shoes with pompoms over the toes could be seen. Pearls dangled from her ears and a locket with her mother's photo hung below her neck on a gold chain. There were eighteen roses in the bouquet from which *ruta* attached to narrow silk ribbons streamed to the floor. The veil which accented her dark hair and youthful face had a long train that she carried over her arm to keep from tripping.

Joe wore a single-breasted dark suit, a rose in his lapel, and a white shirt with a high starched collar that completely covered his neck. The white tie was knotted in front where the collar

"PEARLS DANGLED FROM HER EARS."
Ona married Joe on February 14, 1916

joined, and the neatly folded handkerchief in the top pocket of his suit coat had been recently purchased from the "palace store."

    After the church service, Ona's sister Margaret probably invited friends and relatives to her flat, where she served chicken, purchased alive from a farmer. She would have killed and cleaned the chicken with her own hands, and roasted it in the oven of her new stove. Margaret may also have prepared and served Lithuanian *suris* (fresh farmers' cheese), *desra* (sausage), *kugeli* (potato pudding), dark rye bread, and sauerkraut.

"AFTER THE CHURCH SERVICE, ONA'S SISTER
MARGARET PROBABLY INVITED FRIENDS . . . ."
Standing: Unknown, Vincent Valatka, Miss Kulpanaite, Augustas Kubilius
Seated: Mr. Arentas, Ona Guzeviciene, Juozas, Margaret Valatkiene

Ona moved to Worcester to live with Joe in his flat at 495 Ward Street. (The house has since been torn down to make room for the Massachusetts Turnpike.) To supplement Joe's wages they took in men boarders, recent immigrants from Lithuania, who paid one dollar a week to stay in their home. It was not easy for Ona to feed the men, wash their clothes, and make daily trips to the store to buy the beer they drank at the end of the day when they returned home tired and disheveled from their twelve hour workday.

Joe and Ona's first son was born November 20, 1916. He was baptized at St. Casimir's Lithuanian Church and was named Albert, after Prince Albert of Belgium. Their second son, named Vytautas in honor of the great Lithuanian emancipator who lived in the fourteenth century, was born August 13, 1918.

"JOE AND ONA'S FIRST SON WAS BORN NOVEMBER 20, 1916."

The author's husband, Albert, and his mother

"Their second son [was] named Vytautas . . . ."
Albert and Vytautas (Vic), c. 1923

They lived in Worcester until 1919 after World War I ended and Joe lost his job making steel wire at the Worcester plant. Ona begged him to move back to South Boston. Margaret's husband, George, heard there was a need for workers at the Domino Sugar Refinery where he worked. Joe was hired to tend the machine that washed sugar imported from Cuba.

Chapter Thirteen

A New Beginning

The story of how Joe, Ona, and their children lived in South Boston was related to me by my husband, Albert. "We moved from Worcester to South Boston and lived in a flat at 853 East Fifth Street with my aunt and uncle Valatka. My parents later rented a flat on O Street, which was a rat-infested tenement. I still recall my mother chasing and killing rats with a broom. We left this place very quickly and moved to 625 East Eighth Street, South Boston, on the second floor of a house owned by the Marks family, friends of my parents. The house was about two blocks from the waters of Dorchester Bay, a part of Boston harbor

❖

"We are not certain when my mother's brother Augustas Kubilius arrived in America from Lithuania. It doesn't seem likely that he traveled with my mother Ona on her journey to America, because she never mentioned to any member of our family that he was with her. Also, because of World War I he may not have been able to find a ship from August 1914 to 1919 to carry him across the Atlantic Ocean.

"Upon Augustas Kubilius's arrival he attempted to Americanize his name, so he called himself Gus Kobylis. He met and married a young Lithuanian woman from Hazleton, Pennsylvania, who spoke English fluently. Ana Matuleviciute, Gus Kobylis's bride, became the interpreter for the entire Kubilius family who emigrated to America as well as for a large number of other Lithuanian immigrants who had not learned to speak the English language. We called her Auntie Koby.

❖

"My parents asked Auntie Koby to accompany me to school and enroll me in the classes. During the enrollment Auntie had difficulty spelling Guzevicius, and eventually the teacher, using a phonetic sound equivalent to the name Guzevicius, said that

"... MY MOTHER'S BROTHER AUGUSTAS KUBILIUS ARRIVED IN AMERICA."
Standing: Augustas, Ona Kubiliute, Mr. Rubinskas, unknown, Vincent Valatka
Seated: Margaret and Vincent Valatka with Elinor, c. 1915

they would call me Albert Gustaff, which has been my name to
this day.

❖

"Fortunately, from the Immigration and Naturalization
Service at the United States Department of Justice in Washington,
D.C., I received copies of my father's Declaration of Intention and
his Petition for Naturalization

"On April 15, 1919, my father, Juozas, had filled out his
Declaration of Intention for citizenship, and signed his name as
Joseph Guzievyc.

"October 26, 1921, my father entered his Petition for Naturalization, which had been witnessed by Peter Plansky, a relative,
and Joseph J. Kengris, a friend who worked in the sugar factory in
South Boston. The Petition stated that Juozas's wife, Annie (Ona),
had been born on September 15, 1890, in Lithuania. His two

"HIS TWO CHILDREN, ALBERT AND VYTAUTAS (VIC),
WERE BORN IN WORCESTER, MASSACHUSETTS."
Albert, Ona, Joe, Vic, c. 1923

"WE TRAVELED BY TRAIN ON THE BOSTON AND MAINE RAILROAD TO MONTREAL, CANADA . . . ."

Juozas's son Albert, Antanas, Ona, Juozas, Jonas's wife Jule and son Charles, Jonas, Vytautas (Vic), c. 1931

children Albert and Vytautas (Vic) were born in Worcester, Massachusetts. He renounced all allegiance and fidelity to any foreign prince, potentate, state, or sovereignty, particularly to Russia or any independent state within the bounds of the former Russian Empire. At that time he worked as a ship builder, at the Fore River shipyard in Quincy, Massachusetts.

"After my father Joe's death I discovered the important naturalization certificate among his personal records. The Certificate of Naturalization, No. 1596878, was granted to him on May 8, 1922, at the United States District Court in Boston, Massachusetts.

❖

"About one year after my father became an American citizen," my husband, Albert, continued to say, "he decided it was time to buy a car. I remember that car. It was a Model A Ford, a four-door sedan. We traveled to church on Sunday mornings, to the Franklin Park Zoo on Sunday afternoons, and in the fall after a rainy day we traveled to the woods to pick mushrooms.

"We made many trips to the country to visit our cousins, the Blazis family, who lived on a farm in Stoughton, Massachusetts, where we'd pick potatoes, apples, cucumbers, pears, beets, carrots, and blueberries. My mother bought eggs and cheese. She hand plucked the feathers from the chickens she also purchased.

"I especially enjoyed the overnight stays when we slept in the hay loft in the barn. Everyone, children included, stayed up late into the night telling old-country stories and singing Lithuanian folk songs.

❖

"We traveled by train on the Boston and Maine Railroad to Montreal, Canada, to visit my father's brothers Antanas and Jonas. Antanas had emigrated from Lithuania to Canada but never married. Jonas, who had also immigrated to Canada, married Jule Bazyte. They had one son Charles.

"I especially remember the trips to Canada since my mother would conceal a bottle of Canadian whiskey in her corset when we prepared to return to our home in Massachusetts. Prohibition existed in America at that time, and liquor was unavailable for purchase anywhere in the states. Travelers who were on the way into the United States from another country were forbidden to possess or carry alcoholic liquor.

"My parents were concerned that their possessions might be searched at the border between Canada and the United States, but we were fortunate. No one ever detected the whiskey bottle my mother had hidden within her clothing.

"My father worked in the Fore River Shipyards on the Aircraft Carrier Lexington until the year 1927, when he began to build his home in Mattapan, Massachusetts. My mother worked at Walworth Foundry, a company that manufactured brass valves and faucets, making sand cores to form molds for brass castings. The work was difficult and her hands bled from cuts and bruises. Even though it was forbidden, she'd smuggle into the building a small whiskey bottle filled with kerosene to pour on the cores for easier molding."

"HIS FATHER PURCHASED LAND AT 27 TAMPA STREET IN MATTAPAN AND PROCEEDED TO ERECT A NEW HOUSE."

Albert and Vic stand on the steps of the new house, c. 1928

Albert went on to tell me that his mother became very ill with rheumatic fever and doctors suggested that his parents live farther away from the ocean. His father purchased land at 27 Tampa Street in Mattapan and proceeded to erect a new house. He made sketches of the building he desired and hired an architect to make the blueprints. The house was built during the years 1927-28, Joe doing much of the work himself. Albert and Vic also helped, gaining practical experience that benefitted them and other family members for many years afterward.

The house was built of wood that was stained a dark brown. Brick steps led to the front door, which opened into a hallway with entrances to the living-room/dining-room/sun-room on the right and to the kitchen directly ahead. The second floor held three bedrooms and a bathroom. Another bedroom was in the attic. And the house was centrally heated throughout!

❖

In front of the house Ona and Joe planted a privet hedge and a rosebush which reached the windows of the enclosed sun-porch, the most popular room in which to relax and entertain visitors. Joe also found time to plant a vegetable garden in his small back yard.

Ona's first stove in the kitchen of her new home was a coal stove with an attached two-burner gas range. This early coal stove was later converted to burn kerosene. The cast iron grating, through which the ashes from the burnt coal would drop down to the ash pit at the bottom, was removed from the stove, and in its place two oil burners were installed. Copper tubing carried oil from an inverted heavy glass jug set upon a pedestal mounted about two feet away, a safe distance from the side of the stove.

About 1936 Joe began to do well economically. He purchased a new oil stove for the kitchen. The converted coal to oil stove was relegated to the basement where Ona cooked jellies and preserved fruits and vegetables. Joe also bought a refrigerator, a radio in a cabinet console, and a washing machine. He received substantial discounts since he worked at General Electric, where he made all these purchases.

"ONA PURCHASED A RACCOON FUR COAT . . . ."
Ona Guzeviciene and Margaret Valatkiene, c. 1925

Ona purchased a raccoon fur coat and became a fashion-ably dressed woman wed to an immigrant from Lithuania who worked sincerely and eagerly to prosper in their new country.

She also bought a dining room set with rococo designs. A china cupboard displayed the dishes she collected each week at the movie theater, where they were given away as premiums to at-tract patrons. The manager of the theater presented each woman with either a dinner plate, a cup, a saucer, or a soup plate to make up a set of china, in order to encourage attendance at the theater to view the films. Ona had to attend every week for approximately one year until she collected the complete set of dishes. She talked often about Eddy Nelson and Jeanette McDonald, her favorite stars. Of course, she meant Nelson Eddy.

Although rheumatic fever had damaged Ona's heart, she was happy baking apple pies and *pyraga* (raisin bread) in the oven of the sparkling clean, recently purchased, light gray oil stove in the kitchen of her newly built home, but she complained often that in the new house she had to wash twenty-three windows.

Their neighbors, Mr. and Mrs. Damusis, who also had emigrated from Lithuania, became their good friends. This was fortunate for Ona, since she never learned to speak English fluently, even though she understood many words. Joe attended school in America only one day, but he could read English and spoke the language fluently, although with a deep accent.

The United States plunged into economic depression in 1929. Joe's work hours at the General Electric foundry in Everett were reduced, and eventually they were terminated.

A baker, an immigrant from Lithuania, hired Joe to sell dark rye bread, *pyraga*, cake, and cookies from a truck that Joe himself drove around the streets of South Boston. Joe also papered walls, painted woodwork in homes of friends, and did other odd jobs to sustain his family.

Ona cleaned offices in a building on Beacon Street in Boston. She reported to work at 6 p.m. and traveled home at midnight, always on the streetcar. Eventually Joe returned to his employment at General Electric, where he worked until he retired.

Joseph Guzievyc registered for Social Security on November 27, 1936, and received number 029-05-9993. (The registration form was found among his other personal papers after he passed away.) According to the form, Joe was living in the home he had built at 27 Tampa Street, Mattapan, Massachusetts, and was working for General Electric. He wrote his birth date as August 25, 1892, and that he was born in Suvalki, Lithuania, a district in which Punskas is located. I don't know why he omitted the name Zovoda, which he had originally informed us was his village in

"JOE RETIRED FROM HIS JOB AT [THE] GENERAL
ELECTRIC [FOUNDRY, EVERETT, MASSACHUSETTS]."
Two managers and a superintendent celebrate Joe's career. Joe is second from left, c. 1959

Lithuania. We have learned that Zovoda was such a small place
that the name might not be much used for official purposes.

❖

Ona's heart became weaker each day and in the summer of
1958 the doctor advised us to admit her into New England Memorial Hospital where, within a few short days, she lapsed into a coma.
Her suffering heart finally broke down, and she left this world on
June 12, 1958. Mr. Casper from Casper Funeral Home in South Boston removed her body from the hospital and prepared it for burial.
Ona's remains were placed into a casket and laid out three days
for viewing, in the living room of the home at 27 Tampa Street.
        Friends and relatives visited. Many brought casseroles of
food, doughnuts, and other desserts. According to custom, each
evening, after all the visitors had departed, Ona's son Albert sat
with his mother's body the remaining hours of the night.

On June 17, 1958, Ona's remains were carried to South Boston to St. Peter's Lithuanian Church. Three priests celebrated the Requiem Mass. Family, relatives, and friends accompanied the hearse to New Calvary Cemetery where Ona's body was interred. After the burial, a collation of ham, Lithuanian dark rye bread, salad, cake, coffee, and *boilo* was served at the Lithuanian Club in South Boston.

After Ona's death Joe retired from his job at General Electric. Joe tried to live alone in the home he had built for Ona, but after two years he sold the house and moved to live with his son Albert and family in Arlington, Massachusetts.

Unfortunately, the dust Joe had inhaled in his work at the General Electric foundry had damaged his lungs severely. On December 22, 1975, he stopped breathing. His lifeless body was viewed by his many friends and relatives at Casper Funeral Home in South Boston.

The weather was bitter cold and snowing hard—a blizzard of cascading flakes that left Boston buried in high drifts of white powdery snow. On December 24, Joe's burial day, the snow stopped falling, and the sun emerged through the clouds, but the day remained freezing cold.

The roads were icy and treacherous. After the funeral Mass at St. Peter's Lithuanian Church, very few friends could travel to New Calvary cemetery. Joe was interred in the same grave-site with his beloved Ona. It was a sorrowful day, this day before Christmas.

Juozas Guzevicius and Ona Kubiliute suffered through sad final farewells with their parents when they departed from their homesteads and set out to travel to their new strange land. Neither one ever returned to their former homeland. Juozas never again saw the many tall birch trees that sheltered the masonry cottage. Ona never again picked mushrooms in her native land. Juozas (Joe) and Ona (Anna) had made AMERICA their home.

Grandpa's Last Christmas

J ack Deisler, the first grandson-in-law, loved Joe (Grandpa) and enjoyed his visits with him. Before Jack's sudden death from a heart attack in 1984 he wrote the following story in memory of Joe's life.

❖

It was Grandpa's last Christmas, but we didn't know that then. The house buzzed with Christmas Eve activity: dinner being cooked, the table being set, and presents being wrapped for unwrapping the next day. Everybody had a job to do except grandpa and me, so we sat in a corner of the living room, out of the way, and talked. Actually Grandpa talked.

I wish my words could do justice to his deep, soft voice, his rich accent, and the twinkle in his eyes as he reminisced about his childhood Christmases in Lithuania.

At Christmas time in Lithuania it was always very cold and there was always lots of snow on the ground. On Christmas Eve, after a meatless, twelve course dinner (one course for each Apostle), the animals were fed and then the family went to Midnight Mass, called the Shepherd's Mass. Grandpa, as one of the younger sons, had the job of feeding the animals.

In Lithuania, Christmas was considered such a sacred day that no one worked, not even on a farm. All the animals had to be given a double ration the night before. All the animals, that is, except the horses. When I asked why the horses were left out, Grandpa told me a wonderful old folktale.

❖

When God found out that Adam and Eve had eaten the apple, He got very angry. "Eve," He said, "from now on you will have terrible pain when you have babies. Adam, I have a punishment for you too. From now on, everything you eat, you will take from the earth by the sweat of your brow." Then God threw them out of the Garden of Eden and locked the gate. As Adam and Eve walked away, the snake slithered after them.

Every day, Eve would cook and clean and take care of the babies and, after a while, she had a lot of babies. Every day Adam would go into the fields to plow or sow or harvest. One day God decided to visit Adam and Eve to see how they were doing. When He got to the field where Adam was plowing, He saw the snake riding on the plough and making fun of Adam as he worked. This made God angrier than He had ever been. "What are you doing, making fun of Adam? It's your fault he has to work like this. I made a big mistake. I forgot to punish you. From now on you will help Adam with his work. You will do the hardest part, and so that Adam doesn't have to listen to you, I will make you the dumbest animal of all." In that instant, the snake was changed into the first horse. It was in memory of those first farmers, that the horses went hungry on all the farms in Lithuania on Christmas day. The legend also explains why the horses are so fond of apples. When he was sure no one was looking, Grandpa gave the horses a double ration, too. Legend or not.

The next December, three days before Christmas, Grandpa died. His two sons and daughters-in-law, and granddaughters and grandsons-in-law, and grandson, and great grandson came from all over the United States to be in Boston when he was buried on Christmas Eve.

❖

It had been snowing for days but that morning the snow stopped and the sun glared on the bitter cold cemetery. After the funeral everyone came back to the house, and since the airport was closed, settled in for a family Christmas. By late afternoon the snow was falling again, so we lit a fire and told old stories and laughed and sang carols at the piano and went to Midnight Mass.

The next morning we exchanged homemade presents and private treasures. "Now, what can this be wrapped to look like a pencil? Oh, a pencil! Thank you so much, how did you know I needed one?" At Christmas dinner the champagne Grandpa always provided for the toast was there and someone else made sure the box of chocolates Grandpa always offered after dinner was there.

We will probably never all be in the same place at the same time again. But we will remember that Christmas as a particularly happy one. I began this by saying that the Christmas before was Grandpa's last Christmas. I was wrong.

—Jack Deisler

Book Four

Wally and Verna Shierant

THE FRONT PORCH

In a hammock we sit on cushions made
plump from hand plucked goose feathers.
Chevies gramble out of view
on a noisy street studded with maple trees.
Neighbors, friends, strangers, stroll
the swept clean sidewalk
that touches the bannister.
We nurture intimate gossip,
Ponder town events, church
problems, broken romances, unfulfilled
promises, the new flick at the Victoria.
No need for newspapers.

The front porch has left my world.
I sit on a melancholy deck
locked to a baroque garden of daffodils,
hyacinths, Leland cypress.
Faded images of conversations
wash away one by one.
I read the daily newspaper.

LS/G

Chapter Fourteen

A Parade, a Meeting

T he year was 1915. Verna Matuseviciute and Aggie Novitsky each finished rolling their last cigar of the day, left the factory, and were walking down Hickory Street looking for a place to watch the parade. They were both fifteen years old and had already worked five years in the cigar factory on Hickory Street, the past year on the night shift.

"Let's watch the parade on Oak Street."

"No, let's watch on Hickory Street. There'll be a smaller crowd. I'm short and . . . ."

"You're right. We can jimmy up to the front and sit on the curbstone."

Growing up in Mount Carmel, Pennsylvania, was boring. An occasional trip to the ice cream parlor to buy a "birch beer float"—two scoops of ice cream in a tall glass of birch beer—was a thrilling event.

This parade was exciting because the circus was in town. During the past week posters with pictures of lions, tigers, elephants, and clowns were seen on poles and in store windows, announcing the arrival of the Barnum and Bailey Circus.

Verna, petite and vivacious with dark brown hair that tumbled into curls over her shoulders, wore new high-heeled shoes that she had purchased with her most recent paycheck. She kept bending to rearrange her cotton stockings; the elastic garters above the knees had stretched and were slipping down. In contrast, blonde dignified Aggie wore old worn oxfords, and her stockings were attached to a garter belt under the street length petticoat and skirt that covered her long legs. The girls were still wearing their white uniforms with aprons covering the front of their long skirts.

❖

Verna and Aggie had emigrated from Europe in 1903 with their mothers; Verna from Lithuania and Aggie from Southbank, England. When Verna arrived in America she settled with her parents in a patch town in sight of the Locust Summit Colliery where her father worked as a miner. Unfortunately, her father was suffering with miner's asthma. Medication for this was unknown during the days of dirt roads, and early death was commonplace.

Verna's family needed to escape the coal dust of the colliery, so they moved to the town of Mount Carmel, approximately three miles from the patch town where they had originally settled. They rented a home on South Maple Street, where Verna settled in along with her parents, Ona (Annie) and Martinas (Martin), and her siblings John, Joseph, George, Stanley, and Charles.

Verna always believed that she entered the world on March 15, 1899, in Rudamina, a village in the Mariampole region of Lithuania. The date of her birth could never be confirmed because the church in which she was baptized had burnt to the ground and all important papers were destroyed. People of that era remembered important dates by the weather. "Many days the rains they came and floods they made when you were born," her mother Ona, who never learned to speak English, would say to her.

Aggie also lived in one of the row houses on Maple Street. Aggie liked plucky and vivacious Verna; Verna hoped to learn better English from Aggie's British accent.

❖

Aggie, the taller of the two friends, elbowed her way through the crowd at the parade and found a vacant spot. She gently nudged people aside as she made a space on the curb and pulled Verna down to sit beside her.

A roar from the waiting crowd split the air. "Look, Aggie, here comes the parade!" cried Verna, as she grabbed Aggie's arm and turned her about-face to look at the marchers appearing around the corner. Spectators shouted, clapped, and strained to look over shoulders to get a better view. Children waved flags and balloons as they were picked up by adults in order to see over the sea of humanity that pushed up to the front.

The Ringmaster, dressed in a striking outfit of orange, black, and silver, led the parade with precise military movements as he pointed out turns, stops, and starts with his staff. Elephants lumbered along the unpaved streets; neighing horses trotted; women and men aerialists marched in colorful costumes.

Tigers and bears rolled past in cages on carts pulled by mules, accompanied by trainers who cracked long whips in the air while the animals looked fierce and threatening. Midgets and clowns somersaulted into the crowds, danced with the onlookers, and passed out bulletins advertising the performances.

Suddenly Aggie shouted, "There they are already!" She pointed to a group of musicians coming into view.

"Is he there?" Verna asked as she stretched her five-foot frame to look over the marchers passing in front of her.

"Yes, he's leading the band and playing the cornet at the same time."

"Ooh, I see him already. I have to meet him. Aggie, let's go to Market Street where the parade will be ended."

"Verna, don't make games with me yet."

"Aggie, he's for me. I'm gonna marry him."

"Verna, shush! You can't marry him. He's Polish and you're Lithuanian. Your mama and papa'll never let you, and his parents would kick him out the house."

"I don't care. Aggie, I love him."

"Verna, don't say that. You haven't even met him yet."

"I'll meet him today."

They pushed through the crowd and ran to Market Street where they waited for the band. The musicians marched to a stop, broke ranks, and were packing their instruments, getting ready to leave by the time Verna found enough courage to approach the cornet player. An imposing sight in his uniform although only a head taller than Verna, he was blowing the melody of a Sousa march into his cornet, holding the instrument as if he never wanted to let go.

Verna walked up slowly and stammered, "I-I like your band. Do you play much already?"

"We play in the Casino at Maysville Park every Saturday night," he answered, as he held the cornet to his chest and wiped the mouthpiece with a handkerchief he pulled from his pocket. "This Saturday Papa Laine's Brass Band will be at Maysville. Our band'll play polkas during intermission. Can you polka?"

"Oh yes, and I'd like to go already, but I have no way to get there."

"The Shamokin-Mount Carmel trolley [electric trains] stop at Maysville every Saturday and Sunday. We ride the trains. Come along. You may have to stand, though. The trains are always crowded. By the way, what's your name?"

"Veronica Matuseviciute. My friends call me Verna."

"I'm Walter Shierant. Call me Wally."

Wally and Verna were my parents. This much was related to me by Verna. The rest of the story I remember from my early days in Mount Carmel plus snatches of tales passed on to me by friends and relatives.

Chapter Fifteen

Polkas, Movies, a Cornet

I t all happened in Pennsylvania. Wally Shierant, my father, was born on June 26, 1895, to his parents, Jan and Ana Sierant, in Wilburton, Pennsylvania, a patch town lined with homes that were dilapidated shanties built by the owners of the mines. He grew up with five brothers and sisters—Mary, Andrew, George, Kate, and Frank. Wally attended school until the eighth grade when all young men were expected to start work in a coal breaker.

Wally first worked as a "breaker boy." A car, loaded with coal dug earlier by miners, would be hauled to the top of the building and tipped into a chute. The coal would be crushed by machines into smaller sizes and then slide by gravity down to the waiting "breaker boys." These young boys, sitting on seats straddled across the top of the chute, would remove slate, rock, and other refuse as the broken coal rushed down to fill freight cars at the bottom.

Later Wally worked inside the mines, where he dug coal from the walls with a miner's pick. He wore a cap with an acetylene flame lamp on his head as his cart was pulled by mules through tunnels dug deep into the earth.

The work was dirty, and when Wally got home each day he had to wash black filth off his body in the wooden tub that was carried into the kitchen. Water, brought in from the well on the corner and heated in the same copper pot used to boil clothes on wash day, was poured into the tub. As he washed he could never reach his back, and his mother scrubbed it until his skin was raw. The mines were dangerous, but his father's wages were too small to support the needs of the family, and the boys had to work also.

After a day's labor Wally probably did not take part in the games with other young men. He preferred to listen to the polkas and waltzes played on the accordion by his father's friends.

"WALLY BEGGED HIS PARENTS TO LET HIM BUY A CORNET."
Wally and his horn, c. 1921

He traveled to the nearby towns of Lakeside, Shenandoah, and Shamokin to hear music, and even went as far as Philadelphia to hear John Philip Sousa and his band perform. The *Poet and Peasant Overture* by F. Van Suppe, was his favorite selection. I heard him play it on the piano often when I was a child.

Wally begged his parents to let him buy a cornet. "But how'll you learn to play it?" his mother asked. "There ain't no cornet teachers in any town close by."

"I'll teach myself, mom. I know the notes already," Wally answered, "and I'll play for you the polkas that you like."

Wally bought his cornet. He pursed his lips together and blew clear tones from his instrument immediately. He purchased a book which explained where each note was and soon played the polkas to which his mother listened with delight. Then he encouraged his brothers to buy band instruments, and together they formed the first polka band in the region. Wally was the concertmaster of this small but popular group which marched in every parade playing polkas and Sousa marches.

Verna was ten years old when she was put to work rolling cigars in the factory at Hickory and Fifth Streets, three blocks from her home on Maple Street. Her schooling ended when she was in the third grade, since her family needed more income and she was the oldest child. If she had free time she read *True Romances* and *True Story* magazines, which she hid under her bed from brothers who teased her about her passion for love stories.

Saturday night was date night. Every week Wally hiked down the hill to Verna's home and together they walked the few short blocks to Oak Street where they had their choice of five movie theaters: Theatorium, Lyric, Majestic, Valentine, and Arcade. Wally paid a nickel each for both of them to watch the silent moving pictures. These early movies had no recorded sound. Title cards flashed on the screen to convey the dialogue, while a piano or organ gave musical accompaniment.

Wally and Verna might have seen Lillian Gish in *The Musketeers of Pig Alley*, or Blanche Sweet as the telegrapher in *The Lonedale Operator*. They would certainly have seen "America's

"THEY HAD THEIR CHOICE OF FIVE MOVIE THEATERS . . . ."
The Theatorium on Oak Street, c. 1913
(photo courtesy of Hugh A. Jones, Esq.)

Sweetheart," Mary Pickford, who began as a popular child actress in such movies as *The Lonely Villa*, directed by D. W. Griffith the prolific filmmaker who developed narrative cinema into a great art form

According to the book *FILM: An International History of the Medium* by Robert Sklar,[*] "The five-cent theater, beginning around 1905, made movies a part of everyday life for immigrants and working-class Americans."

---

[*]Robert Sklar, *Film: An International History of the Medium* (New York: Prentice Hall: H.N. Abrams, 1993), p. 48.

"... AND SIT ON THE SPINDLY ICE CREAM PARLOR CHAIRS."
An early soda fountain in Mount Carmel, c. 1916

The gripping action in serial films such as *The Perils of Pauline* thrilled Verna. All week long she would sing a poor imitation of the song *"Poor Pauline"* in an off-key but earnest voice as she waited for the next week's episode.

Wally liked Fatty Arbuckle in the Mack Sennett Keystone Kops films, and he sat through double features to see the creative funny antics of Charlie Chaplin in *Kid Auto Races at Venice* in which Chaplin was first inspired to dress as a tramp.

After the movie, Wally and Verna would walk up the street to Romanis's (later known as Langis's) and sit on the spindly ice cream parlor chairs. Wally would order an ice cream soda—a large glass of soda water filled with gobs of vanilla ice cream and topped with whipped cream and a cherry. He always asked for two straws, and he and Verna would sit close together as they shared the cool drink.

In the winter Wally held Verna tight and close as he guided his sled down the crusty snow-covered slope on hilly Maple Street,

"THEY MET AT CHURCH PARTIES AND PICNICS . . . ."
Andrew, Aggie, Verna, Wally, Jenny, and George, c. 1914

"SHE HAD ALREADY DECIDED THAT WALLY WAS THE MAN FOR HER."
Verna awaits her turn as Wally operates the drinking fountain for friends at a park, c. 1916

and the wind they raced against gave their cheeks a rosy glow.

In the spring they met at church parties and picnics where they often wandered off with their friends to play spin the bottle or post office. The games gave Wally the opportunity to put his arm around Verna and peck her on the cheek. Sometimes he even caught her unawares and gave her a resounding kiss on the lips. Verna didn't mind—she had already decided that Wally was the man for her.

"Verna Matuseviciute and Wally Shierant
were married . . . on May 30, 1916."

Wally, Aggie, George, Verna

Chapter Sixteen

The Wedding

Verna Matuseviciute and Wally Shierant were married in Holy Cross Lithuanian Church in Mount Carmel on May 30, 1916. Both their parents were unhappy because they believed that Lithuanian women should not wed Polish men. In Europe there was continual controversy between the two countries over territory, and this engendered animosity between the common people as well as the ruling class.

"You are young, still behind the ears wet," said Ona, Verna's mother. "Sixteen years old only two months already."

"Wally, you the horn play good but a mistake big you make already. Verna's mama and papa don't know no English. That means troubles big, and out the window love flies and dies the marriage," Ana, Wally's mother, said to him.

But this was America, and parents did not have the same influence here that they had in the old country.

A dressmaker made Verna's gown from chiffon tulle fabric and lace. Verna wore a crown made from *ruta*, the Lithuanian national flower and the country's sign of virginity. The soft branches with tiny green leaves gave out a sweet delicate fragrance, and Verna was a tiny vision in white as she walked down the aisle to meet Wally in his best Sunday suit. Aggie was her maid of honor, and Wally's brother George was the best man.

After the religious ceremony, Verna's mother and father greeted the couple with a glass of wine and a dish holding bread and salt, an old-country custom signifying a healthy and prosperous future. They invited friends and relatives to come back to their home to celebrate the wedding.

Verna had baked her own wedding cake—three layers covered with creamy white frosting and fresh coconut. The parents opened a keg of beer—home brewed—and served a dinner of

"MONDAY SHE LAUNDERED THE CLOTHES . . . ."
Verna used a Maytag electric washing machine; her mother, Ana, used a manual washer
(photo courtesy Eckley Miners' Village Museum)

"SATURDAY SHE BAKED PIES AND CAKES . . . ."
A later-model anthracite coal stove
(photo courtesy Eckley Miners' Village Museum)

homemade sausage, sauerkraut, and rye bread.

An accordion player played polkas, and Wally played his cornet. The music was loud. Verna's friends sat in one corner of the room harmonizing Lithuanian folk tunes about young sweethearts who met under birch trees. Walter's friends gathered in another area singing Polish traditional wedding melodies. Wally dispensed *boilo* freely all through the day as guests advanced with gifts of money. In return Verna danced with each gift giver.

When the beer keg was empty the guests began to leave. Friends led the newlyweds to their bedroom and the *ruta* wreath was removed from Verna's head. Women pushed her into the center of a circle as they sang, "*Oi ruta, ruta, rutytele, ko nezaliuoji darzelije*" (Oh rue, rue, little rue, why do you not grow in my garden?). "May the first one be a boy" was heard over and over as the men jostled Wally to the bedroom.

My sister Irene tells me that Verna, our mother, told her the following story:

> "The day after the wedding Verna awoke early in the morning to make a special breakfast for Wally. Her neighbor had informed her that the food men liked most was gefilte fish, and that this was always served on the first day after the wedding. Verna prepared it in the manner she was instructed, frying it carefully so that it would be the right texture (not too hard and not too soft) and placed it in front of Wally with a big smile. Wally took one perplexed look at the dish and said, 'Ain't we got no Pennsylvania scrapple?'"

Housekeeping was the grueling job assigned to women in the early twentieth century, as for countless centuries before, and Verna had an unbreakable routine. Monday she laundered the clothes, boiling white articles in a large oblong copper kettle resting on two burners atop the stove. Three large tubs were carried into the kitchen. The first was filled with hot water in which Verna scrubbed the clothes on a board using a bar of *Fels Naphtha* soap, or soap that she made herself from a combination of lye and the discarded lard and fats of meats. Cold water for rinsing was poured into the remaining tubs, with bluing added to the last rinse. Water was laboriously wrung out of the clothing by hand until a gadget appeared on the market in which two slim rollers turned by a crank squeezed water from the clothing as it was fed between them. Even in the coldest weather the laundry was hung outside to dry on long lines attached to tall posts.

Ironing took place on Tuesday. Flat-irons were heated on top of the stove, and all the laundry, including sheets and socks, was ironed. Wednesdays and Thursdays were spent mending torn items or working in the garden. Friday, Verna cleaned the house. Rooms were swept and dusted, windows washed, beds aired, and the linoleum on the kitchen floor scrubbed until it shone like crystal.

Saturday she baked pies and cakes, three or four of each. There were many kinds. The pies might be coconut cream, huckleberry, or raisin; the cakes might be white, chocolate, or gingerbread. Verna's top favorite was gingerbread, which she served with dollops of rich whipped cream. Her other favorite was coconut cream pie. She tested the oven with a quick turn of the hand to determine if the temperature was just right to make the cake rise or brown the meringue on the pie, and barely was the cake or pie out of the stove than she would eat some of it, hot and juicy. She was never satisfied with one piece but had to eat two or three, and each one with a large dollop of whipped cream. She also baked bread—rye bread, white bread, and raisin bread—which she shared with the nuns at the convent and the priest at the rectory.

Verna learned to make meals that pleased Wally. She pickled pigs feet and cucumbers in a crock, stored boiled eggs in beet juice, made sauerkraut in a wooden tub, preserved chowchow, piccalilli, and strawberry jam. The coal bucket beside the stove was never empty, and vegetable soup, made with inexpensive meatless beef bones and fresh vegetables, simmered on the back burner of the stove every day. The soup was always hot, and when Wally complained that it burned his tongue she'd say, "Ain't you got no wind under your nose?"

The doughnuts Verna made for Shrove Tuesday were the envy of the neighborhood women. She made doughnuts at other times too, whenever she saved some of the raised dough from making bread. She would roll out the dough, cut it into circles with the rim of a drinking glass, cut out the center with the rim of a whiskey shot glass, and then fry the doughnuts in deep boiling-hot fat.

Verna purchased meat, vegetables, fruit, and eggs from farmers who came through town with horse-drawn wagons and shouted "potatoes," "beans," "tomatoes," "carrots," and the names of other country produce as they traveled the streets. She joined her neighbors as they ran from their homes to select from the wagons the food they wanted for their families.

Verna served her meals sometimes on the hand-painted dishes she collected, which were much admired by all her friends and relatives. But her favorite set of tableware was the set of dishes she acquired while going weekly to the Victoria Theater. Occasionally Verna asked me to go to the theater for her. Although I was a child I paid the adult ticket price and convinced the cashier to give me the dish that was awarded that day.

Verna went to the movies often. She never missed a film that starred Rudolph Valentino, her favorite movie star. In desert scenes, dressed in long flowing robes, on his head a turban with flaps reaching gracefully to his shoulders, Valentino was handsome, and he always won the leading lady at the end of the story.

Verna liked the elegant Victoria theater, which opened in Mount Carmel in 1921 and was dedicated in 1923. She enjoyed the large stage, the carpeted floors, the soft seats, the exquisite chandelier in the ceiling of the theater, and the comfortable sofas outside the rest rooms.

The greatest attraction was the new Giant Moller pipe organ as it brought forth sounds of violins, cellos, horns, saxophones, trumpets, drums, and other instruments as it filled the auditorium with popular music of the day. The organ melodies were the highlight of every silent movie. Mr. S.S. Grand, organist, played soft melodic tunes during a romantic scene, loud rollicking music during an argument or rambunctious fight, and melancholy songs for a sad scene.

The *Mount Carmel Item* of Monday, July 9, 1923, published the news about the formal opening and dedication of the Victoria

Theater by Chamberlain Amusement Enterprises, Inc., "in Midland Pennsylvania's most magnificent playhouse at 7:00 and 9:00 o'clock, Monday Evening, July 9, 1923."

The *Mount Carmel Item* reported the following opening program:

1. Prologue (Some interesting facts)
2. "Great Train Robbery." Note - The management has procured this film, which is 20 years old, to draw a comparison between the class of entertainment offered in the old Theatorium at the opening 16 years ago and the present day.
3. Dedication.
4. Overture, "American Fantasy." Mr. S.S. Grand, Organist, at the Giant Moller.
5. Feature Photoplay. Paramount will present Bebe Daniels and Antonio Moreno in a truly modern photoplay - "The Exciters" a play of the trend of today.
6. Comedy, "Dogs of War."
7. Exit March

It was also noted that the theater was constructed at a cost of $300,000, and took more than one year to build. The Giant Moller pipe organ cost $30,000.

"ON OCTOBER 14, 1917, I WAS BORN . . . ."

The author, Leona, about age 4, poses with one of the many maple trees on Maple Street

Wally and Verna rented a row house on Maple Street in Mount Carmel. On October 14, 1917, I was born, Verna's first child, and she named me Leona. After my birth she spent many weeks in bed claiming she was too weak to take up her duties quickly.

By 1920, according to the census of that year, Verna and Wally were residing in a duplex house at 1107 Scott St., Kulpmont, Pennsylvania. Their neighbors on the other side of the duplex were Aggie and Wally's brother Andrew, who met at the same parade and were wed shortly after Wally and Verna's marriage.

On June 6, 1919, in Kulpmont, my sister Veronica came into the world. I was too young to realize that she was born with a defect. The bone in her nose was missing and the skin lay flat on her face. Verna was devastated and blamed herself for this unhappy occurrence. "Why wasn't I more careful when I was pregnant?" she asked. "Wally," she said, "I think it happened when we were watching the parade of soldiers who came home from the war. Remember that guy whose nose was shot off? I thought I would faint already."

Verna traveled with Veronica to many doctors. Plastic surgery was in its infancy and she had difficulty locating a specialist. They made numerous trips together to Philadelphia, where eventually surgery was performed to correct Veronica's problem. A bone removed from Veronica's hip and skin taken from her arm were attached to her nose. Veronica always had a large scar on the inside of her arm where skin for the graft was taken. Veronica's birth defect did not affect her personality. She was sociable, talkative, and popular with everyone.

After some time Verna heard that the house next door to her parents' house on Maple Street in Mount Carmel was vacant and for sale. "Wally, let's buy the house in Mount Carmel," she begged.

"I'm not buyin' nothin'. Ain't you happy here, Aggie next door 'n all?" Wally asked.

"WALLY AND VERNA BROUGHT SIX CHILDREN . . . INTO THE WORLD . . . ."
Standing: Leona, John, Veronica, Irene
Seated: Wally, Verna
Kneeling: Francis, Walter, c. 1934

"I'm sick o' livin' out here in the sticks, and my mom'll help me with the kids."

Wally and Verna bought the house, and they opened a variety store where they sold flour, sugar, bread, cigars, cigarettes, and ice cream. I still remember reaching into a sparkling glass showcase for penny candy. They charged buyers "on tick," writing in the customers book the amounts of purchases made to be paid on payday. This business venture was not successful. Customers were delinquent in payments, and many did not pay at all.

❖

On June 25, 1921, Verna gave birth to her first son, John. Four years later on August 17, 1925, a daughter Irene was added to the family. In all, Wally and Verna brought six children—three boys and three girls—into the world: Leona, Veronica, John, Irene, Francis, and Walter, Jr.

All the babies were born in the second floor bedroom of the home in which the family was living at the time. Verna's pregnancies were normal. She experienced natural births with no medication and nursed all her children. "You must eat for two people, you and the baby," Verna was advised by friends and relatives. She had no difficulty obeying, lost her slim figure, and never regained it.

Chapter Seventeen

Wally, the Organist

A round 1919, Wally and Verna bought a piano—a large used Lester upright—so that Wally could continue to make music. He couldn't afford to pay a teacher, so he bought an instruction book and learned to move his fingers over the keys in a simplified version of *Poet and Peasant Overture* that he practiced daily.

When I was four years old, Wally led me to the piano and put my finger on middle C; and I found all the notes above and

"WALLY AND VERNA BOUGHT A PIANO . . . ."
A Lester upright piano like Wally and Verna's, and a radio of the era
(photo courtesy Eckley Miners' Village Museum)

"THE PASTOR OF THE LITHUANIAN CHURCH ASKED
WALLY TO BECOME THE ORGANIST . . . ."
Wally at the organ, with a few members of his choir, c. 1939

below. I asked him to teach me but he refused. "I never took no lessons and I don't know how to teach," he said, as he played *Poet and Peasant Overture* for what seemed to me the hundredth time. "We'll look for a teacher when you grow up."

Wally began to play well, was asked to play the organ in St. Joseph's Polish Church, and often sang during the services at Holy Cross Lithuanian Church

❖

In 1920 Father Bartuska, pastor of the Lithuanian church, asked Wally to become the organist and choir director at the Holy Cross Church until a person who spoke Lithuanian could be hired. Wally accepted. Another organist was never located and, with the exception of a brief interlude when he was organist in Girardville, Pennsylvania, Wally held this position until a few years before his death.

Little by little he built a choir that not only sang in Holy Cross Church but gave concerts each year in the ballroom of the very popular amusement park, Lakewood, on August 15, Lithuanian Day. Emma Kelminski had studied voice for many years and led the soprano section. Stanley Petruskevicius was endowed with a pleasing tenor voice and sang with Wally often, especially during church holidays. Wally became popular among the Lithuanian people and learned to speak a few words in their language.

Saturday evenings Wally and Verna baked the wafers to be distributed for communion at the Sunday Masses, a chore given to all Lithuanian organists. Before making the wafers, Wally and Verna made certain that the kitchen was immaculately clean, dishes washed and put away neatly into the cupboards, the floor scrubbed thoroughly, then waxed and polished to a smooth glossy surface. Pots were hung in place behind the stove, and a fire burned bright with new coal carried up from the bin in the cellar.

Verna made a paste of water and flour which Wally poured into a waffle iron made up of two small oval irons attached to long handles and embossed with religious themes. Wally heated the irons on top of the stove, and as he pushed them together with the mixture inside, a round thin wafer resulted. Verna, pressing down the wooden handle of a sharp cookie cutter on the wafer, formed the many small round wafers that would be distributed to the congregation for Holy Communion the next day at Mass.

❖

Wally and Verna enjoyed this time together, chatting about the news of the day and speaking in endearing terms about their life together with their children and friends. I recall walking into a warm happy kitchen during those moments and feeling a sense of comfort and peace.

In 1926 on Easter day I awakened to a strange sound—music reverberated throughout the house. A choir was singing *Pulkim ant Keliu* (Fall on Your Knees), a hymn sung in the Lithuanian church at daily Mass. I raced down the stairs to see my father, Wally, standing beside a rectangular cabinet about four feet high, and as he turned a crank on its side beautiful melodies flowed into the rooms. My siblings joined me quickly, and we spent the entire day turning the crank on the side of the Victrola. We listened to the *Poet and Peasant Overture,* Sousa marches and *Pulkim ant Keliu,* as we put on the turntable again and again the few records my father had purchased

Chapter Eighteen

The Model T Ford

About 1927 Wally stopped working at the mines, became an agent for the Metropolitan Life Insurance Company, and bought his first car, a Model T Ford. In order to start the Tin Lizzie, his favorite name for the car, Wally would spin the crank in front of the engine. As the motor caught he'd jump behind the wheel and roll merrily on to his destination.

He drove his family to outings every weekend at Lakewood or Lakeside Park, where they met and conversed with friends from Mahanoy City, Tamaqua, Shenandoah, or Minersville. They always began those trips early in the morning so that they could reserve a table by placing on it a large picnic basket filled with chicken, ham, potato salad, coleslaw, pickled beets, fresh bread, and huckleberry pie—all of which Verna had prepared the day before.

They swam in the pool, rode the roller coaster, and rode with their children on the merry-go-round. Everyone brought pinochle playing cards, and "You trumped my ace!" "You lost that trick!" or "I'll never play with you again!" could be heard all over the park.

Wally used his Ford to collect the weekly premiums from his customers and to visit the many farmers who invested in the insurance he sold. At the farms he was often invited to partake of one of his favorite foods, salt pork served with tomatoes picked in the gardens the day before. The salt pork , which was 75% fat, was placed on a slab of dark homemade rye bread, and the tomato was eaten on the side. Verna often traveled with Wally. It gave her an opportunity to buy *suris* and fresh churned butter.

❖

In 1927 Father Valanciunas, pastor of St. Vincent Lithuanian Church in Girardville, Pennsylvania, asked Wally to come to his parish to direct the choir and play the organ for the services.

Wally moved to Girardville, but he continued his work as an insurance agent. Each morning after singing the Mass he drove the half hour back to Mount Carmel to collect the weekly premiums his customers paid for the insurance they had purchased from him.

Wally and Verna's first home in Girardville was a two-story row house located in an alley. The house, which contained two bedrooms, a living room, and a kitchen, with an outhouse at the end of a small back yard, faced the rear of the church. Wally awakened five minutes before church bells signaled the beginning of Mass and he still managed to have time to smoke one of his ever-present cigarettes before he started to sing.

After a few months Verna heard of a larger house available for rent. "Wally, a real bathroom there is already; we must move."

"Verna, ain't you satisfied? Fifteen minutes I'll need to walk to church already."

"Wally, stretch your brain a little out and see we can't live in the sticks."

❖

They moved to the house that had plumbing and an indoor bathroom. Verna was happy. In the bathroom on the second floor hot water, heated by the furnace in the cellar, flowed out of a gray tin spigot at the top of a long narrow tub held up by four iron claw feet. Next to the tub was a metal sink. Beside the sink was a toilet that was flushed by pulling a metal chain hanging down from a water-filled tank attached to the wall above the commode. Wally admitted that he didn't mind standing outside the door waiting his turn to use the new bathroom. This was more convenient than using an outhouse at the end of the yard, and there was no need to fill the wooden tub in the kitchen with hot water to bathe each Saturday night.

❖

Their new neighbors were the Chikotas family, who had a very well established business distributing beer and soda. They became good friends, drinking beer and playing pinochle together many evenings.

Later that year, Adam Chikotas purchased a box from which music and words were heard at the same time that they were performed in distant places. "Wally, come to hear my new radio," he invited.

"Can I bring the kids?" Wally asked. We climbed over the bannister to the front porch next door and marched into the house. As we walked in I heard the words, "Ladies and gentlemen, this is the largest gate in the history of boxing. Walking into the ring in a scarlet red dressing gown is the ever-popular ex-marine, Gene Tunney. Hear the ovation he is getting! Listen to the tumultuous sound of cheers!"

I looked around searching for the owner of the voice but there was no one in the room. The sound was coming from a brown box about two feet high and shaped like a semicircle at the top. In the center was a small lighted opening with numbers and a round knob underneath. "And in his royal blue dressing gown Jack Dempsey climbs into the ring, but his reception is different. Listen to the boos," continued the voice in the box.

The year was 1927, the day September 22. We heard a blow by blow description of a fight in which Tunney outboxed Dempsey until the seventh round, when Dempsey floored Tunney. But Tunney arose at that famous long count of nine and went on to win the fight.

Beautiful melodies began to flow from the strange box. I heard an orchestra playing Schubert's *Unfinished Symphony*. I sat back to enjoy the sound of violins, cellos, and horns when suddenly the music stopped. "I'm sorry, we can't listen to this. We must wait for Sunday," said Mr. Chikotas as he turned the knob and the box was silent.

"Mom, ask him to play that nice music," I whispered into Verna's ear.

"Now, Leona, you know that children should be seen and not heard," Verna replied, and that settled the matter. Frustrated and baffled, I climbed back over the bannister to the porch of our home.

❖

Wally and Verna lived in Girardville about two years. Their fifth child and second son, Francis, was born September 28, 1928, in the bedroom on the second floor of the house with the new bathroom.

But Verna was not pleased living far away from her friends and familiar haunts in Mount Carmel. She learned there was a need for an organist in the Lithuanian church, so she urged Wally to return to his former position in the Holy Cross church.

Wally was content to play the organ at the Holy Cross Lithuanian Church again, so Wally and Verna moved back to Mount Carmel. He saw that he would be living closer to his insurance clients and would not have to continue those daily trips from Girardville to Mount Carmel to collect their weekly fees. The travel had become lonely and boring. There also was never sufficient time to return to Girardville to partake of the noon meals in which Verna constantly made certain his favorites were available.

Chapter Nineteen

1929 - The Stock Market Crash

T he stock market crash of 1929 produced repercussions that were felt all over the world. Banks were closed and the Great Depression soon followed. Many of Wally and Verna's friends lost all their possessions—their money, their houses, their cars. New jobs were not available, and very many old jobs disappeared.

Wally continued to play the organ and collect weekly payments from his insurance clients. In many cases it was only 25 cents. Life insurance remained precious to everyone who had it, even during those difficult years. Although Wally's income was lessened, he was still able to feed his family and buy necessities.

Verna fed hoboes, transients who traveled from town to town looking for work. Many rode into town in boxcars on trains that stopped at the railroad station on Market Street. The hoboes appeared on the steps in Verna's back yard begging either for food or for a dime to buy a cup of coffee. She never gave money but would instead go into her kitchen and put together a meal for them. She contended that they wanted the dime to buy whiskey, and she had no intention to pay for liquor of any kind.

During the Great Depression in the United States, dance marathons were the rage. Couples danced day and night. A cash prize was awarded to the last couple that remained standing. It was a crazy time. Employment was scarce. Some participants danced in order to receive the hot meals given at intervals. Performers would fall asleep while their partners endeavored to hold them up. Verna and Wally enjoyed attending dance marathons at Lakewood Park, to place bets on the couples they thought would have the endurance to be the last pair dancing in the marathon.

They also placed bets on flagpole sitters. Men fashioned seats on tops of poles and lived in the chairs without climbing down for days, even for weeks. It was a desperate time.

Verna and Wally were happy when President Franklin D. Roosevelt introduced the New Deal and, in 1935, created the WPA (Works Progress Administration, later renamed Work Projects Administration), which gave jobs to the unemployed. They began to see young men leave the area to build roads and develop parklands.

Chapter Twenty

239 West Fifth Street

During the depression Verna and Wally lived in Mount Carmel with Verna's mother Ona on Maple Street. In 1932 on Christmas day, about one o'clock in the morning, their last son, Walter, Jr., was born while Wally was playing the organ and directing the choir at Midnight Mass. I had gone to Mass with my father and had been singing with the choir but actually had attended the service so that I would be there to play the organ if Wally needed his cigarette.

My father had lived up to his early promise to find a piano teacher for me. E. May Wardrop, having studied at the New England Conservatory in Boston, Massachusetts, was expert at teaching the piano, and she lived in Mount Carmel. Miss Wardrop became my teacher, and I practiced diligently.

The organ in the Holy Cross Church was available and I began to perform on it. I never became proficient at playing the pipe organ, but I played the hymns well enough that when my dad had his desperate need for a cigarette I was a willing substitute to help at the organ.

At that Midnight Mass in 1932, the choir sang unusually well; the carols were more beautiful than ever. I failed to notice that my father had not given the invitation he usually gave at each Midnight Christmas Mass for the members of his choir to come to his home afterward and have some of the delicacies that Verna would have prepared for them. In addition to the coconut cream pies, chocolate and coconut cakes, raisin and rye breads, cookies and candies, Verna would have roasted a large ham, which she would serve with her own pickled beets, chowchow, and relish. Christmas breakfast was a delicious feast.

At the end of the Mass my father Wally and I walked the small distance home together. We greeted friends and hummed the melodies that were just performed in church. I looked forward

"WALLY AND VERNA WERE PLEASED WITH THEIR NEWLY REMODELED HOME."
The proud owners stand in front of 239 West Fifth Street, c. 1945

to reading the books I expected to discover. No library existed in Mount Carmel, and literature for avid readers was hard to get. My mother would not disappoint me, was my thought. She always bought books on this special holiday.

I also looked forward to decorating the Christmas tree with the ornaments that my parents had collected through the years. At last I was old enough to take part in this task. I knew that I would carefully put pretend icicles all over the branches of the green tree that I knew had been in a pail of water at the bottom of the steps under the back porch.

The tree was never transported into the living room until Christmas eve. Wally and Verna thought they had hidden it well, but my sisters and I had searched until we found that beautiful harbinger of delicious and exciting days to come. We savored our discovery and never let on to our parents that we knew the hiding place.

After the tree was fully decorated that year I would be permitted to help my parents place all the gifts under the tree. Gifts for the family were never wrapped. They were placed in organized piles under the Christmas tree so that each child would know which gifts were his or hers.

The children always arose early on Christmas morning and rushed down to see what Santa Claus had left for them. There were gifts of clothing—pajamas, socks for all of us, blouses for girls, shirts for boys, a jacket or coat for my sister Irene who had outgrown her hand-me-downs. We also found toys—a bike for Johnny, a sled for Fritz (Francis), a new doll each for my sisters Veronica and Irene, and books for me.

Socks that we children had hung near the stove in the kitchen would be filled with fruit and nuts, a coloring book, pencils, paper, and always a nickel, a dime and a few pennies at the bottom of the sock. As we grew older we may also have found a quarter in our sock.

❖

But on that early Christmas morning in 1932, as my father and I entered our home, there he was—a new brother, a tiny red-faced baby I was not happy to see. I wanted to say, "Take him back where he came from." I was angry. How could Verna, my mother, have another baby when I was so old, all of fifteen years of age. Also, I never knew that a new child was on the way. My mother managed to keep secret her physical condition even as she gained much weight.

"Pick him up," my mother urged.

I stormed out of the room in tears. I didn't wish to decorate the Christmas tree. I was devastated.

My sister Veronica, in the meantime, picked up the baby, stroked his little hands and feet, and spoke to him softly. Walter, Jr., became the joy of the family.

Shortly after the birth of Walter, Jr., Wally and Verna bought a home at 239 West Fifth Street in Mount Carmel. It wasn't long before Verna became dissatisfied with her new home. A bathroom in the house to replace the outhouse was imperative, so remodeling was begun. The stairs were moved from the side to the back of the dining room, and a long hallway was put in on the second floor to reach the new bathroom that was added above the back porch. Verna and Wally were pleased with their newly remodeled home.

Verna enjoyed relaxing in the swing on the front porch. It didn't hang from the ceiling like those of her friends and neighbors, but rather had sturdy legs which stood on the floor of the porch and held up the framework. Large comfortable cushions filled with goose feathers and down, and covered with rainproof fabric, were placed on the seating area.

From her seat on the swing Verna conversed with neighbors and friends who passed by along the sidewalk. She also looked forward to meeting Scheuren, the milkman, as he brought fresh milk to the house each day. The milk in those days was pasteurized but not homogenized, and when it arrived, Verna would immediately pour off the cream from the top and whip it until it was creamy enough to put on top of her freshly made gingerbread.

Every second or third day she watched for the iceman, to escort him into the kitchen, where he would put a block of ice into a compartment in the icebox.

Evenings she joined other mothers who met in each others' homes to sew newly designed quilts. Each woman made quilts for her family, and Verna crafted some for herself as well as for each of her children.

This was the time to catch up on the news of the day. The women talked about the special prices in grocery stores and informed each other when sales in clothing stores were about to occur. They exchanged recipes and spoke about their friends who were ill and those who were getting married. Since only a few could read easily, the friendly quilters were not interested in world news, and they preferred to receive local news by word of mouth. The evening was filled with gossip.

Verna's women friends were never encouraged to read, and even the few who had a little education found reading difficult. Husbands instructed their wives how to vote and related to family members the important news in the town newspaper. Women were informed that a woman's place was in the home having babies, washing clothes, cooking, and doing other household tasks. Wives were ordered not to venture into a man's territory where all the decisions of the family must be made. It was unthinkable that a woman should contemplate or desire any type of higher education.

Verna, however, loved to read, especially the *True Story* magazines that were popular at that time. She perused the *Mount Carmel Item* daily. Wally and Verna had many arguments during voting season. Verna often convinced Wally to vote her way.

❖

Easter was a day of celebration. Verna always baked a large ham over which she had poured a bottle of ginger ale to bring out a more enticingly delectable taste. On Easter morning we, the children, awoke to find a dining room table covered with baskets stuffed with chocolate candy eggs and rabbits purchased at Langis's candy store. The baskets also held farmers' eggs that had been boiled and colored the day before, and Verna's popular homemade sweet chocolate-covered Easter eggs.

Holy Mass was early—about 6:00 A.M. Everyone was bedecked in a new outfit—for the girls a new hat, gloves, and purse, and a flower corsage. After enjoying a dinner of Verna's homemade bread, ham, country vegetables, salad and a fresh coconut-frosted white cake, we joined the Easter Parade on Oak Street.

"[For Easter,] everyone was bedecked in a new outfit . . . ."
Veronica and Irene model new dresses made by their mother, c. 1940

We had spent a dreary snow-filled winter and a Lenten period of fasting. To walk on a beautiful sunny street and observe the new garments was a joyful spectacle of color and pleasure. Some mothers had labored for days to dress each of their children. Nobody mistook the members of any family in which each child's outfit matched her siblings' colorful clothing.

❖

Oak Street was the main shopping avenue in Mount Carmel. A clothing store, drugstore, gift store, hardware store, and grocery store were in a row of adjacent buildings. Penney's, a large department store located on the corner of Oak and Fifth Streets, sold men's and women's underwear and outerwear, children's clothing, sheets, blankets, and curtains.

Verna bought fabrics at Guinan's, furniture at Shimock's, jewelry at Kessler's, shoes at Kinney's. All important occasions were recorded in photographs at Akelaitis Photo Studio. Wally purchased his shirts, ties, and suits at Lanuskey's Men's store. Langis's served the best ice cream sundaes and candy, but it was the most expensive, so instead the soda fountain at Nesbitt's drug store was the most popular place on the street. Here customers sat on high stools in front of a counter across which they could see the sodas being poured and topped with large scoops of ice cream. This establishment stood on the opposite corner from the Guarantee Trust Bank.

Everything was priced under one dollar at Newberry's. But at Woolworth's, the five and ten cent store, a dime was the most Verna paid for any article.

❖

The stores were located on three short blocks, from Sixth Street to Third Street where, if you stood on the corner, you could see the Victoria Theater a short half block away. On Saturdays Verna gave each one of us, her children, a dime to go to the matinee, which featured all the latest films.

There was much excited conversation when advertisements appeared with information that "talkies" were coming to the theater. In 1927 the first talking film, *The Jazz Singer,* arrived at the Victoria. Long lines of movie-goers filled the street beside the box office. Everyone in town wanted to see the first show.

The theater was filled quickly. There was a hushed expectancy. An electric silence filled the air until suddenly the words Al Jolson spoke rang through the auditorium. *"Wait a minute. Wait a minute. You ain't heard nothing yet."*

This was an amazing, almost unbelievable experience, especially when Jolson sang his famous song *My Mammy*. In the film, Jolson bent to his knees and stretched out his arms as he sang words that would become very familiar to us. Not many Mount Carmelites had had the joy of seeing and hearing him in person. No more would we need to make long expensive trips to Philadelphia or New York City to see and hear famous performers. The moving pictures would bring them to us.

Many of us walked out of the theater that day humming the tune of *My Mammy*. But I don't believe anyone could foresee the true meaning of those first audible words in this very popular medium, moving pictures: *"Wait a minute! Wait a minute! You ain't heard nothing yet."*

❖

In 1935, after much controversy, I entered Marywood College in Scranton, Pennsylvania. Verna and Wally's friends and neighbors had been displeased that I was considering a higher education. "Why does she need to go to college, she's only a girl." "She doesn't need college to get married and have a baby." "Save your money for your sons." "Wait and you'll see, she'll bring home a bundle in a blanket and there'll be no father." My parents listened to all the remarks but decided that I should have a college education.

At first, Verna and Wally were distressed because they didn't know how they would pay for tuition, living expenses, and books. "I could stop drinkin' beer," Wally remarked.

"If only Father Koncius would give you the money he owes you, we might be able to afford to let her go to school," Verna remarked. "He's given you no money for three years, not even for singin' the funerals, weddings, and the daily Masses. Why don't you talk to him already?"

"Now, you know I did, Verna. He always says that he'll pay next month."

As it turned out, Father Koncius found an answer to Wally and Verna's problem of how to pay for Leona's college education. Through his influence, I was awarded a college scholarship which paid for all expenses. (Later Dr. Koncius claimed that this paid his entire debt to Wally.) I enrolled at Marywood in 1935 and graduated *cum laude* in 1939 with a Bachelor of Music degree. I was also the recipient of the O'Reilly Medal, an honor awarded only to an outstanding music student and performer.

❖

My sister Veronica also attended Marywood College, but she was unhappy at the school, and after a year she transferred to St. Mary's Hospital in Reading, Pennsylvania, where she studied to be a nurse. Friends and neighbors were more willing that Veronica should be educated, because they believed her disfigurement could cause a problem to her future. Moreover, the world needed nurses.

Johnny won a football scholarship to Bridgeton Academy in Bridgeton, Maine. He later transferred to Boston College. Fritz received a football scholarship to Wake Forest College in Pennsylvania. Fritz attended Wake Forest College less than a year, since he felt that the circumstances presented to him were not what he had been promised.

The children were growing up quickly and leaving home. Wally and Verna were beginning to get lonely. "I miss Leona and her piano playin'. The house is empty without her playin'. These days when I dust the piano all I see in my mind is Leona sittin' on the stool turnin' her music pages," Verna said to Wally.

"I miss Veronica meetin' me at the door when I come home after collectin' the insurance money. She always said, 'Hi daddy, gimme your coat. I'll hang it up'," Wally added.

". . . YOU'RE MY HALF-BROTHER AND I HAVEN'T SEEN YOU FOR FIFTY YEARS."
Wally, Granddaughter Joanie Gustaff, and Joe Boder, in Mount Carmel, c. 1956

Chapter Twenty-One

Joe Boder

O ne Evening In June 1949, as Verna and Wally were relaxing after dinner, the doorbell rang with three sharp blasts
and one long incessant sound. "Answer the door, Walty,"
Wally shouted to his youngest son, who opened the door to see an
elderly man, a stranger. After a few words with the visitor Walty
called out, "Hey dad, there's a guy here who says he wants to talk
to you. He says his name is Joe Boder." Verna and Wally rushed to
the front door. "What did you say your name was?" asked Wally
of the stockily built man at the entrance to the house. "If you said
you're Joe Boder, you're my half-brother and I haven't seen you for
fifty years." "That's me," answered the stranger, "I've been gone
for fifty years." "Come on in!" "Can I bring my suitcase?" Wally
noticed the luggage beside the door.

Jozef Boder (his name in Galicia) remained for twelve years
in Mount Carmel, until his death on August 6, 1961. The first evening that he returned he related how he had left his mother when
he was in his twenties and that he had joined the United States
Navy and later the merchant marine. He was now retired and
wanted to live near members of his family.

At first he lived with Wally and Verna. It was not long before Verna became disenchanted with his drinking and smoking.
"Wally, tell your brother to leave. I get scared when he comes
home late at night drunk and fallin' all over the porch. Tell him
to get a room by himself somewhere. No one can put up with his
drinkin' and carousin'."

"Joe, you better find another place to live. Verna's mad,"
Wally told his half-brother. Joe rented a room on Third Street, but
he visited Verna and Wally often. Joe enjoyed Verna's meals.

"JOHN . . . ENLIST[ED] IN THE COAST GUARD[;] . . . VERONICA
ENTERED THE ARMY . . . IN THE RESERVE NURSE CORPS."
Veronica and John in uniform, c. 1942

Chapter Twenty-Two

The Second World War

In 1939 the Second World War began in Europe, and Frank-lin Roosevelt, president of the United States, announced that young men would be inducted into the armed forces. In 1941 Wally witnessed his son John leave Boston College in his sopho-more year and enlist in the Coast Guard. On August 10, 1942, his daughter Veronica entered the army as a Second Lieutenant in the Reserve Nurse Corps. She left the service before the end of the war because frequent asthma attacks were undermining her health.

Families throughout the country were required to ration food, gasoline, and other items needed for the war effort. Wally felt a need to help in some measure, so he raised turkeys. Verna tended a garden, planting tomatoes, beans, carrots, and lettuce. The days were sad and long. Wally and Verna feared getting that telegram which so many parents received, informing them that their offspring had been killed or was missing in action.

In 1949 Fritz (Francis) entered the navy. He served until 1950 and received an honorable discharge since he too suffered from asthma, a debilitating condition that plagued him most of his life.

On January 10, 1951, Wally saw his youngest son, Walter, Jr., enlist in the Navy. When Walter was honorably discharged on October 20, 1954, he displayed two stars on his battle ribbon, which signified that he was in the war zone off the coast of Korea.

Walter's enlistment in the armed services involved many risks. In his reminiscences about those times, he told us that in one instance when he was helmsman of the aircraft carrier *Oriskany*, he barely avoided being blown up by a mine. He was at the wheel, steering the ship, with earphones over both ears in order to receive

"WALLY FELT A NEED TO HELP [THE WAR EFFORT] . . . , SO HE RAISED TURKEYS."
Wally and friends, c. 1943

instructions from the captain. Suddenly he heard "RIGHT FULL RUDDER," repeated urgently again and again. He quickly turned the ship to the right and barely escaped hitting a mine floating on the ocean waves. The captain had tried to alert him about the danger moments before, but the noise from planes taking off had drowned out the sound of the captain's voice. Walter saved the ship by his quick response.

On another occasion Walter lost a very good friend. A plane was returning from a bombing mission over Korea. One bomb was still attached under the plane and could not be released. The pilot circled the carrier, desperately trying to dislodge the bomb, but he could not. Finally, the captain made the very difficult decision to permit the plane to land on the ship. The plane landed. The bomb came loose, bounced three times, and exploded just before it reached the ammunition area.

Walter was on "condition watch" (on deck as an observer). He saw his photographer friend run to take pictures and fall back from the blast of the explosion into his face. As the photographer fell he dropped the camera. Walter dashed into the area, retrieved the camera, and turned it over to the officer of the deck. The film of the explosion was shown later on newsreels in theaters all over the world, but Walter had lost his good friend. The exploding bomb had killed the courageous photographer instantly.

❖

In 1962 Mount Carmel celebrated the Centennial Anniversary of the town. Mount Carmelites were encouraged to dress in the attire of those who had lived there a hundred years before. Verna resurrected her old sewing machine and designed outfits for herself and Wally. They then joined the picturesque processions that were proceeding down Oak Street. Those who had dared to join the groups in modern dress were apprehended and confined in a makeshift prison for a short time.

"IN 1962 MOUNT CARMEL CELEBRATED [ITS] CENTENNIAL ANNIVERSARY . . . ."
Verna and Wally display their spirit in homemade costumes

Verna and Wally enjoyed wearing their old-fashioned outfits when they walked from their home on Fifth Street to Oak Street, the main shopping area. They were delighted to meet friends and neighbors who were attired as they were. Verna and Wally even took time to visit the make-believe jail to urge the occupants to join in the fun by finding and wearing apparel similar to that of a century before.

❖

"Wally, you better go see Dr. Lustusky. You don't look so good," Verna told him one morning as they were having a breakfast of Pennsylvania Dutch scrapple and coffee with Verna's home-baked rye bread.

"You better stop smoking, Wally," Dr. Lustusky said after an extensive examination. "How many cigarettes do you smoke a day?"

"Maybe one to two packs. I've been smokin' since I've been a kid about ten years old."

"Well, if you don't stop now you'll be dead in a month. Your heart's in bad shape."

Wally stopped "cold turkey," but the smoking had taken its toll on his heart. February 11, 1966, three months before Wally and Verna's fiftieth wedding anniversary, Wally passed away in the middle of the night at Geisinger Memorial Hospital in Danville, Pennsylvania.

The organist from St. Vincent's Church in Girardville played the organ at Wally's funeral, and Wally's faithful choir sang the Requiem Mass. Many relatives and friends gathered in their cars and followed the hearse that carried his body up the Merriam Mountain to the Lithuanian cemetery where he was buried in the family plot.

Verna continued to live at 239 West Fifth Street. Her children had all married and moved away from the family home. I was in Massachusetts. Veronica, Irene, Fritz, and Walter lived in Southern California. Johnny remained in Mount Carmel and resided a few blocks from her house.

❖

"You're gonna get it from mom," my brother John was calling me on the phone from Mount Carmel. "She's angry with you that you put her in the hospital." Verna had cancer of the lymph glands. She was being medicated and, although we didn't know it at the time, she was having a disturbing reaction to the drugs the doctor had prescribed. John could not cope with all the attention she needed, and he had asked me to come down to help.

I made weekly visits to Mount Carmel, traveling by plane each weekend from Logan Airport in Boston to the Avoca Airport between Scranton and Wilkes-Barre.

After many conversations with Dr. Jushinsky, her physician, and conferring with Verna, we decided a nursing home was the only solution. She could never be left alone. Although she was too weak to stand she would insist upon getting out of the bed by herself. We often found her on the floor unable to move.

She had been in the nursing home in Frackville just three days when she broke her arm. The nursing attendants had put gates on the sides of her bed to prevent her from attempting to get up, but she climbed over the top and fell to the floor. She was moved to the Ashland Hospital.

"Leona, please play the organ at the Mass for my funeral." I was visiting Verna at the hospital where she was nursing her broken arm.

"Mom, I don't know if I'll be able to."

"Oh yes, you will. Sing the hymn, *Mother at Your Feet is Kneeling* and the *Ave Maria* that I like, also."

While she was giving me those orders I saw her eyes fill with tears. "I tried to be a good mother," she said, "But I made many mistakes."

"You did the best you could," I told her. "There is no one in the world to teach parents how to raise children. Your sons and daughters are all living nicely, raising their own families, working well to support themselves, and always staying in touch with you."

"Yes, I know this, but are they happy? Will they remember that I tried to be a good mother?"

"Mom, I love you. You were a good mother."

I departed from the hospital carrying the small piece of chicken she urged me take from her dinner plate. As I turned around to look at her she was sitting in the wheelchair at the end of the corridor waving to me. This was our last goodbye.

The time had arrived to alert my brothers and sisters that they should visit if they wanted to spend some time with Verna while she was still living. Irene and Fritz visited for one week. Veronica and Walter came after they left.

When Veronica arrived in Mount Carmel Verna was back in the nursing home. At their first visit Verna was distraught and uncomfortable. Veronica saw that her mouth was full of food she could not chew so she cleaned out her palate and fed her only liquids. She also insisted that the attendants give morphine to Verna to relieve her of the unbearable pain with which she was suffering. Verna was comfortable enough to converse the first few days, but she gradually fell into an unwakeable slumber.

"I feel I must stop giving her water," Veronica told me over the phone. "She has been unconscious for a few days and I'm only prolonging her life." We both agreed it was a wise decision even though we realized the consequences. Verna was ill beyond medical help, and suffering much.

The next day Walter and Veronica visited Verna. Walter told me that as they were both standing by the bed speaking softly they noticed a change in Verna.

Suddenly, Veronica said, "Walter, she's dying."

"Mom, I love you," Walter said to Verna as he watched her facial color turn from pink to gray.

"She heard you, Walter." Verna had squeezed Veronica's hand.

❧

On October 30, 1972, Verna departed this world. For many years she had fought the ravages of cancer of the lymph glands. Before her death she made arrangements for all her children to come to her funeral, which she had planned herself. On the pretext that she would wear the gown to my daughter's wedding a few months earlier she had asked me to make a blue satin dress in her size. She lay in this blue confection in a casket at the Lucas Funeral Home and, at her bidding, I remembered to play the organ and sing her favorite hymns at the Mass.

She was buried next to Wally in the Lithuanian cemetery on the top of Merriam Mountain where together, in their early years of marriage, they had picked huckleberries and mushrooms.

Tell Me That You Love Me

The building rumbled
with rollicking steps
and juvenile sounds
I was six
"Make her learn,"
was all I heard

At six plus twelve
you packed my bag
A slap on my hip
your hard bosom
pressed to my breast
"Read your books,"
I heard you say

Over my head
slithered the gown
and the veil
the scent of roses
a wet kiss
a stingy hug
"Make him happy,"
you said with a grin

Like a statue you lie
in that icy white bed
My hunger bursts
you do not speak
Tell me
that you love me.

LS/G

Singing The Tears

W e entered the room nervously, all six of us. Incense mingled with the scent of roses, carnations, and chrysanthemums filled the air. I led the strange procession, followed by my brothers and sisters.

A large silver crucifix hung on the wall, and copper candlesticks, four feet high, stood at the head and foot of the open ornamented rectangular casket we encountered as our eyes became accustomed to the darkness that greeted us.

We stood beside each other in a straight line in front of the open box which was lined inside with white satin fabric. Verna lay in it as if she were asleep.

"She looks nice," John's words broke through the silence.

"Yes, so much at peace," Veronica said in a tired voice. She had hardly slept the past two weeks taking care of her in her illness.

"She lost a lot of weight." Walter had not seen her for some years, since before the cancer had begun ravaging her body.

"Her face looks very natural, but I don't like the way they fixed her hair. She never wore it like that. It's not becoming," Irene muttered into the tenseness in the room.

"Did you order the dark rye bread and the raisin pie?" Fritzi was concerned about the needs of people who would be attending the various services. "We can't have a funeral without raisin pie in this coal region of Pennsylvania. It's the custom."

My thought was that she lay there with a pale unnatural look and a forced smile. "Can she see us?" My words were soft and unintelligible. "Will she like the service we prepared for her?"

Not one of us cried at that moment. Ten years had passed in which we hadn't seen each other, and we were becoming friends again. Our only contact was that woman lying in her deep unwakeable sleep. Today we would greet relatives and friends who'd be attending the services.

As I stood there and studied her countenance more closely, I was startled. Am I dreaming? Did I see her lips move? Is she trying to give us a message? What does she want to say? She always felt it was her duty to give advice to her family and friends. Will she somehow continue to teach us how to confront life?

My sister Irene interrupted my concentration. "Is this the dress you made for her, Leona?"

"Yes, I made the dress for her to wear to Ronni's wedding. She lost a lot of weight and I had to guess at her measurements. I used a pattern for a size twelve."

"Everything matches. The burning candles and the white satin lining accent the folds and the blue shade of the gown. I believe mom would have been happy with the arrangements made for her viewing," Veronica said as she joined us. "Did she wear the dress to the wedding?"

"She looked like a grown up teenager with premature gray hair when she modeled the outfit on her visit to my home about eight months ago. She seemed to enjoy the twelve hour trip in the Ford that she made from her home in Pennsylvania to our home in Arlington, Massachusetts, but when the wedding day arrived she was too ill to attend. She tricked me into making the gown for the wedding. She always planned to be dressed in it at her death."

Walter's friends had left and he joined us near the white satin lined casket. "I remember that Saturdays with mom were spent in the kitchen. She liked to cook. Every week she baked pies and cakes and never made only one of each."

"She liked to make gingerbread and coconut cream pie." Our brother John had returned from a meeting with Lucas, the undertaker. "I remember the delicious aromas in the kitchen. I could barely wait to taste the cake or pie she was baking. She was a good cook."

"Yes, and that's why she was always overweight until she got the cancer," Fritzi, overhearing the conversation, added with some sadness.

I recalled that baking was done in the oven of the stove that burned coal. She brought buckets of coal up from the bin in the cellar and kept the fire embers alive at all times. It was not easy to fill the bucket with coal, carry it up the stairs, pour the black nuggets into the burning hot embers, and with a quick toss of the wrist in the oven determine when it was hot enough to bake.

Suddenly I understood the message that motionless body was relaying to me. *Who was going to sing the tears?*

My mother, who had emigrated from Lithuania with her parents, had still practiced old-country customs. Her firm belief had been that at the viewing of a dead person someone had to stand in front of the lifeless body and sing the tears of the family. She was always determined that this ritual take place, and if there was no one from the immediate family to perform, she'd sing the tears herself for the bereaved. It didn't matter whether she knew the departed one—to sing the tears was a custom not to be denied.

My memory traveled back to the years when I was a teenager and John Lucas, the husband of mother's friend Anna, had passed away. John suffered miners' asthma for many years before he stopped breathing earthly air.

Mother stood in front of Mr. Lucas's casket and, in a wailing tone of lament, weaving the upper part of her body from side to side, she asked the dead one, "Why did you die? Why did you leave your wife and children? The days are sad and long since you are not here. The bed is icy cold. Your toes aren't warming the toes of your companion. Who'll be there to say good morning to your wife when she awakens? Who'll be there to wipe her tears when she cries? Who'll rake the leaves in the fall and plant the potatoes in the spring? Your wife and children are crying for you. They call your name and you don't answer. The raisin pies will taste like sawdust. You aren't here to enjoy them. Why did you leave this world and the people who love you?" She'd chant the words over and over again.

We, her embarrassed children, argued about who could stop her. We'd attempt to pull her away from the casket or whisper into her ear to be quiet, but we were not successful. Nothing worked. She always "did her thing." We noticed that when she went into her grieving song no one interrupted, and the house was filled with loud uncontrollable sobs. The next day a stream of people came to thank her for her performance.

"Farewell, sweet mother, family treasure. Through you we've had a glimpse of tradition. Today we'll ride with you to the church and the cemetery. There's no one to sing the tears, but I'll sing *Mother at Your Feet is Kneeling*, your favorite hymn, during the service in church. As you are lowered into your last resting place the choir will sing *Amzinaji Atilsi duok mirusiems Viespati*, I whispered to the motionless figure as all six of us stood again in a straight line in front of the open casket with the powder puff vision of white and blue.

Friends and relatives streamed out of the funeral parlor saying their last good-byes to the inanimate one in her last sleep. I turned to Fritzi who was standing beside me. His eyes were filled with tears. "Don't worry, Fritzi. The raisin pie was ordered."

"And don't forget the Lithuanian dark rye bread."

Verna's Recipes

Verna dictated recipes from her memories to Irene Shierant/Wascavage

Chili Sauce

1 lug *tomatoes*	2 Tbsp. *salt*
1 large bunch *celery*	2 c. *sugar*
2 lbs. *onions*	¼ tsp. *chili pepper*
3 *green peppers*, seeded	½ tsp. *black pepper*
3 *red peppers*, seeded	½ tsp. *cinnamon*
1 c. *vinegar*	½ tsp. *allspice*

Peel tomatoes. Put tomatoes, celery, onions, and peppers through a food chopper. Add remaining ingredients. Bring to a boil and boil until tomatoes are soft. Put mixture into sterilized jars and seal.

Chow chow

Tomatoes	*Yellow string beans*
Celery	*Salt*
Lima beans	*Vinegar*
Small onions	*Water*
Red pimento or chili peppers	*Sugar*
Cauliflower	*Yellow mustard*
Pickles	¼ tsp. *turmeric*

Cut up all kinds of vegetables in small pieces. Salt them. Let stand for a while. Boil ½ water and ½ vinegar. Drain the vegetables and put into the boiling brine. Add sugar to taste. Bring to a boil again. Add mustard to taste. Add turmeric. Fill sterilized jars with hot chow chow and seal.

Coleslaw

1 med. head *cabbage*	2 Tbsp. *sugar*
1 glass (8 oz.) *sour cream*	½ tsp. *salt*
1 glass (8 oz.) *mayonnaise*	*Paprika* or *pepper*
½ glass (4 oz.) *vinegar*	

If cabbage is dry (in winter) cut it in half and let stand in cold water about 10 minutes. Drain well. Shred cabbage finely. Mix sour cream, mayonnaise, vinegar, and sugar, and add to shredded cabbage. Let stand 10 minutes. Salt to taste. Sprinkle paprika or pepper on top. The dressing must be a little more sour than sweet because the cabbage will take it up.

Whole Pickles

Cucumbers (select ones that are short and fat with small seeds)	*Whole allspice*
	Oleander seeds
Salted water to cover	*water*
Fresh dill	*vinegar*
Garlic cloves	*salt*
Bay leaf	

Cover cucumbers with salted water. Let stand 1 hr. Wash off with cold water and dry with cloth. Pack into hot, sterilized jars. Add dill, garlic, bay leaf, allspice, and oleander seeds. Combine water, vinegar and salt (for 2 gal. water, use 2 c. vinegar and 1 c. salt). Boil all of this together and then pour on cucumbers in jars, leaving ¼ in. airspace Put lids on jars loosely and place jars in hot water bath until cucumbers change to a yellow color (keep water bath on a low flame to keep water hot). Tighten lids. Don't eat pickles for 2 months. Put in refrigerator overnight before eating.

Doughnuts

Combine and allow to stand at room temperature until bubbles begin to form:

2 cakes *yeast*   ½ c. *water,* lukewarm
4 tsp. *sugar*   ½ c. *milk*, lukewarm

Make a light batter from:

1 qt. *milk*, lukewarm   3 c. *flour* (or more)

Add yeast mixture to batter and let rise ½ hour or more. Cream together:

½ lb. *margarine*   6 *egg yolks*, slightly beaten.
2 c. *sugar*   (reserve the whites)

Stir the margarine mixture with the batter. Combine:

5 lbs. *flour*   *Grated orange* or *vanilla*
1 tsp. *salt*

Gradually add flour mixture to the batter to form a soft dough (stop adding flour mixture before dough becomes stiff). Knead dough, then fold in with your hands:

6 *egg whites*, beaten.

Put dough in a greased bowl and let it rise until twice the size - punch down and let it double in size again. Take small amounts at a time and stretch by hand, to 1 inch thick, and cut into doughnut shape (use water glass to cut circle and whiskey shot glass to cut out center). Place on greased pans and let rise about 1 hour. Fry @ 350 degrees for about five minutes or until brown.

Easter Eggs

1 fresh *coconut*
½ lb. softened *butter* mixed with
½ pt. jar *marshmallow cream*
　　　or
3 heaping Tbsp. *peanut butter*

1½ lb. *confectioner's sugar*
Unsweetened chocolate

　　　Grate coconut. Let stand 2-3 hrs. on paper towel. Combine coconut with butter mixture or peanut butter. Add enough sugar so that it will not be too sweet. It will take less sugar if you let the coconut dry a while. Mix well. Form mixture into egg-shapes. Let the eggs dry a few days. Then dip them into melted unsweetened chocolate. Put on waxed paper to cool.

Pyraga (Raisin Bread)
(recipe courtesy of Vincent Kudirka)

5 pkgs. dry *yeast* or 5 oz. fresh
yeast
3/4 c. warm *water*
3 c. *milk*
1½ c. *sugar* (12 oz.)
3 tsp. *salt*

3 boxes *golden raisins* (3 lbs.)
3 sticks *margarine* (3/4 lb.)
3 sticks *butter* (3/4 lb.)
8 *eggs*
5 lbs. *flour* (all-purpose or bread)

　　　Dissolve yeast in warm water. Scald milk. Add sugar, salt, and raisins, and soak for 5 minutes. Melt butter and margarine. Beat eggs until yellow and frothy. Combine all ingredients in a large bowl and mix well until dough forms a ball. If dough is too soft, add a little more flour. Set dough in large greased bowl, cover with clean kitchen towel and let rise for about 1½ hours or until it doubles in size. Punch dough down and let sit for another 1½ hours. Take dough and scale off 2½ lb. pieces. Form into loaves and place into well greased pans. Let rise until one inch over pan. Bake @ 350 degrees for 30 minutes, then bake @ 325 degrees for one hour. This batch makes five large loaves (9" x 5" pans) for 2 ½ lbs. or 6 small loaves (8" x 4" pans) for 2 lbs.

Rye Bread

2 c. *rye flour*	1 to 2 Tbsp. *salt*
1 qt. boiling *water*	1 Tbsp. melted *shortening*
1 Tbsp. *caraway seeds*	¼ c. *vinegar* (scant)
1 cake *yeast*	2 Tbsp. *sugar*
½ tsp. *sugar*	7 c. *white flour*

Night before: Bring 1 qt. water to boil and pour over 1 c. rye flour. Let stand until it cools off. Add caraway seeds. If mixture seems too thick, add more lukewarm water until mixture has a sticky consistency. Dissolve yeast and ½ tsp. sugar in ½ c. lukewarm water. Let stand all night. (This gets sourish.)

Next morning: To the rye and caraway mixture add the yeast mixture, 1 c. rye flour, salt, melted shortening, vinegar, and 2 Tbsp. sugar. Gradually add white flour, kneading the dough until it is quite sticky. Put dough in greased bowl. Allow to double in size. Punch down and shape into loaves. Put in greased loaf pans and let rise. Bake at 350 degrees for 60 min.

Glossary

back burner - the burners on a coal stove that are not directly over the burning coal

burners - removable round iron plates in the stove top upon which pots are placed to cook the food

boilo - whiskey boiled with herbs

breaker - plant for crushing, cleaning, and grading coal

buddy - miner's helper

colliery - coal mine and its connected buildings

cornet - a brass instrument resembling a trumpet but having a shorter partly conical tube

culm - coal screenings discarded at the breaker

feather tick - comforter hand-filled with goose feathers and down

gulag - the Soviet system of concentration camps and prisons

huckleberry - a kind of small blueberry that grows wild in Pennsylvania

kielbasa - Lithuanian-style sausage

kugeli - potato pudding

lug - a shallow rectangular shipping container for produce

markes - old Lithuanian land measure, approximately 1.25 acres

mociute - grandmother

on tick - purchased on credit until earned salary was received to pay the debt

partisanas - partisans; guerilla freedom fighters

patch town - coal mining town with housing built by the mine owners

pyraga - raisin bread

Prothonotary - chief court clerk

ruta - rue, a fragrant flowering herb, the Lithuanian national flower

ship-card - ticket for ocean passage

suris - fresh "farmers' cheese"

zloty - the Polish currency

Maps

Family Trees

Family Tree of Juozas and Ona Guzevicius

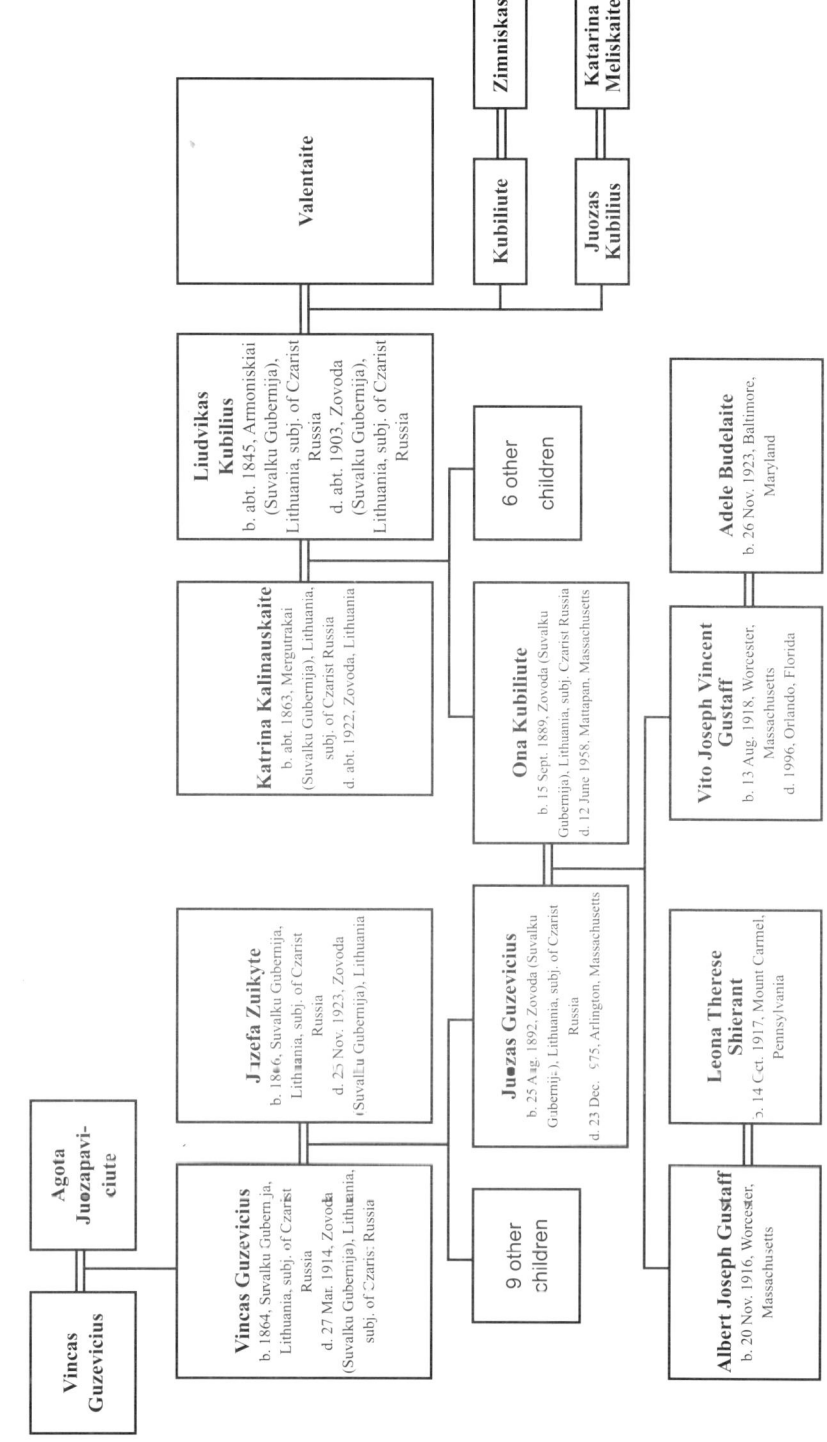

Family Tree of Martinas and Ona Matusevicius

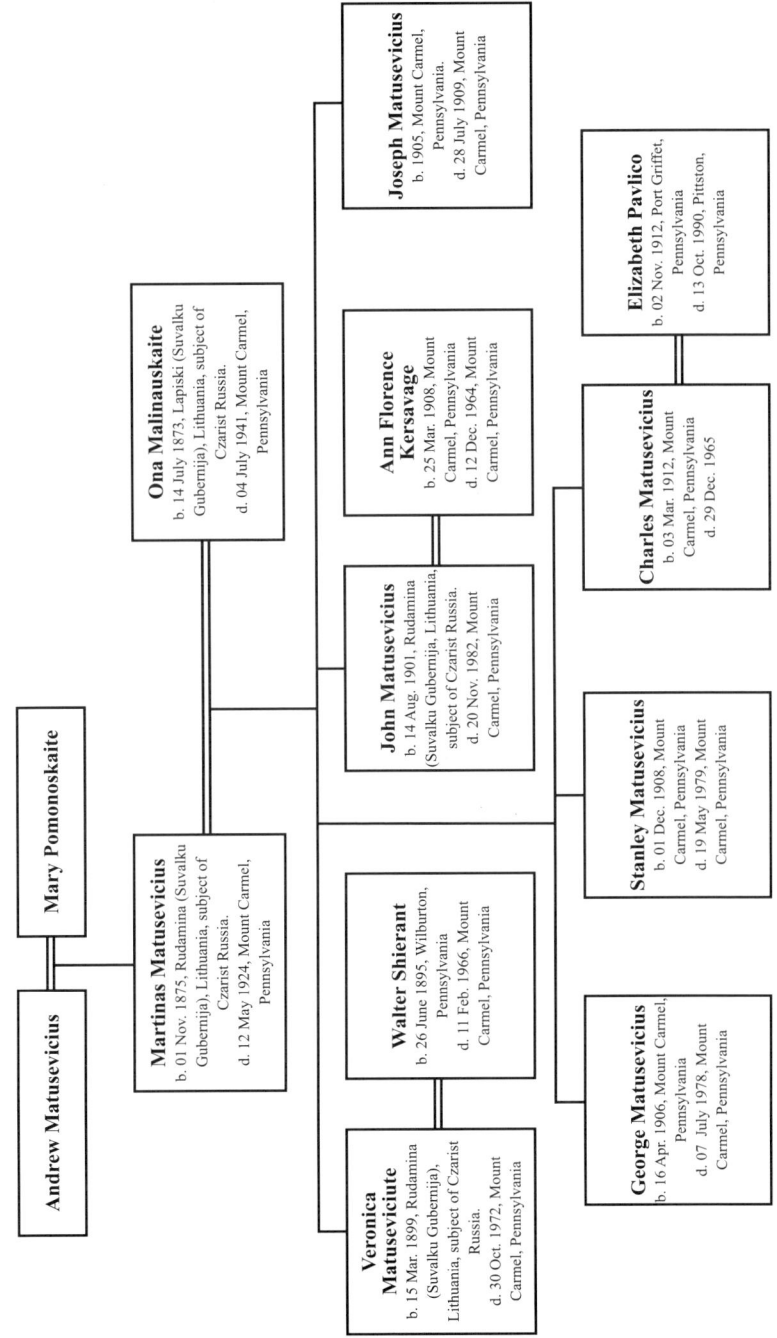

Family Tree of Wally and Verna Shierant

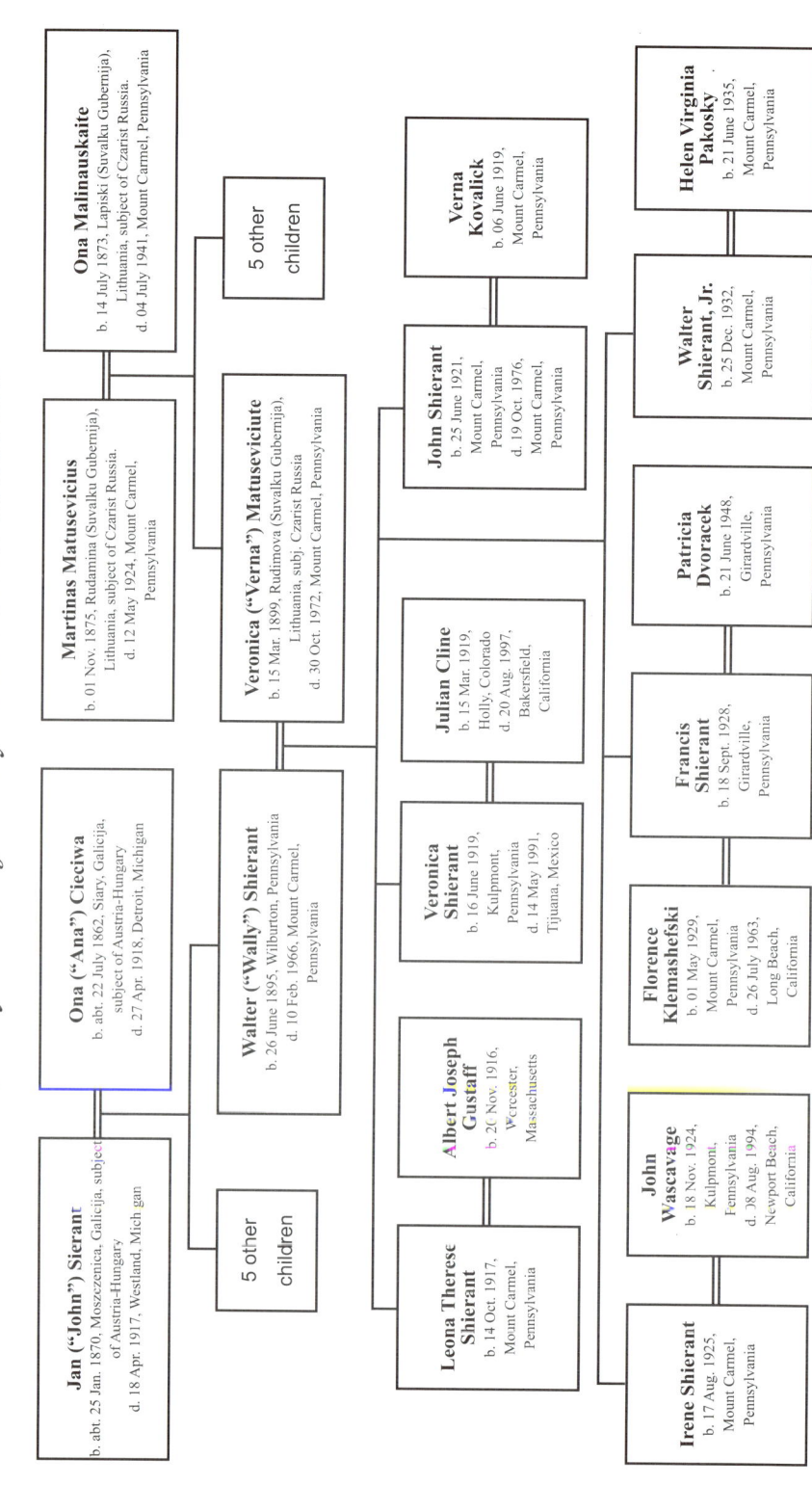

Ona ("Ana") Cieciwa
b. abt. 22 July 1862, Siary, Galicija, subject of Austria-Hungary
d. 27 Apr. 1918, Detroit, Michigan

Ona Malinauskaite
b. 14 July 1873, Lapiski (Suvalku Gubernija), Lithuania, subject of Czarist Russia.
d. 04 July 1941, Mount Carmel, Pennsylvania

Martinas Matusevicius
b. 01 Nov. 1875, Rudamina (Suvalku Gubernija), Lithuania, subject of Czarist Russia.
d. 12 May 1924, Mount Carmel, Pennsylvania

5 other children

Verna Kovalick
b. 06 June 1919, Mount Carmel, Pennsylvania

Helen Virginia Pakosky
b. 21 June 1935, Mount Carmel, Pennsylvania

Jan ("John") Sierant
b. abt. 25 Jan. 1870, Moszczenica, Galicija, subject of Austria-Hungary
d. 18 Apr. 1917, Westland, Michigan

Walter ("Wally") Shierant
b. 26 June 1895, Wilburton, Pennsylvania
d. 10 Feb. 1966, Mount Carmel, Pennsylvania

Veronica ("Verna") Matuseviciute
b. 15 Mar. 1899, Rudimova (Suvalku Gubernija), Lithuania, subj. Czarist Russia
d. 30 Oct. 1972, Mount Carmel, Pennsylvania

John Shierant
b. 25 June 1921, Mount Carmel, Pennsylvania
d. 19 Oct. 1976, Mount Carmel, Pennsylvania

Julian Cline
b. 15 Mar. 1919, Holly, Colorado
d. 20 Aug. 1997, Bakersfield, California

Walter Shierant, Jr.
b. 25 Dec. 1932, Mount Carmel, Pennsylvania

Patricia Dvoracek
b. 21 June 1948, Girardville, Pennsylvania

5 other children

Albert Joseph Gustaff
b. 20 Nov. 1916, Worcester, Massachusetts

Veronica Shierant
b. 16 June 1919, Kulpmont, Pennsylvania
d. 14 May 1991, Tijuana, Mexico

Francis Shierant
b. 18 Sept. 1928, Girardville, Pennsylvania

Leona Therese Shierant
b. 14 Oct. 1917, Mount Carmel, Pennsylvania

John Wascavage
b. 18 Nov. 1924, Kulpmont, Pennsylvania
d. 08 Aug. 1994, Newport Beach, California

Florence Klemashefski
b. 01 May 1929, Mount Carmel, Pennsylvania
d. 26 July 1963, Long Beach, California

Irene Shierant
b. 17 Aug. 1925, Mount Carmel, Pennsylvania

Family Tree of Jan and Ana Sierant

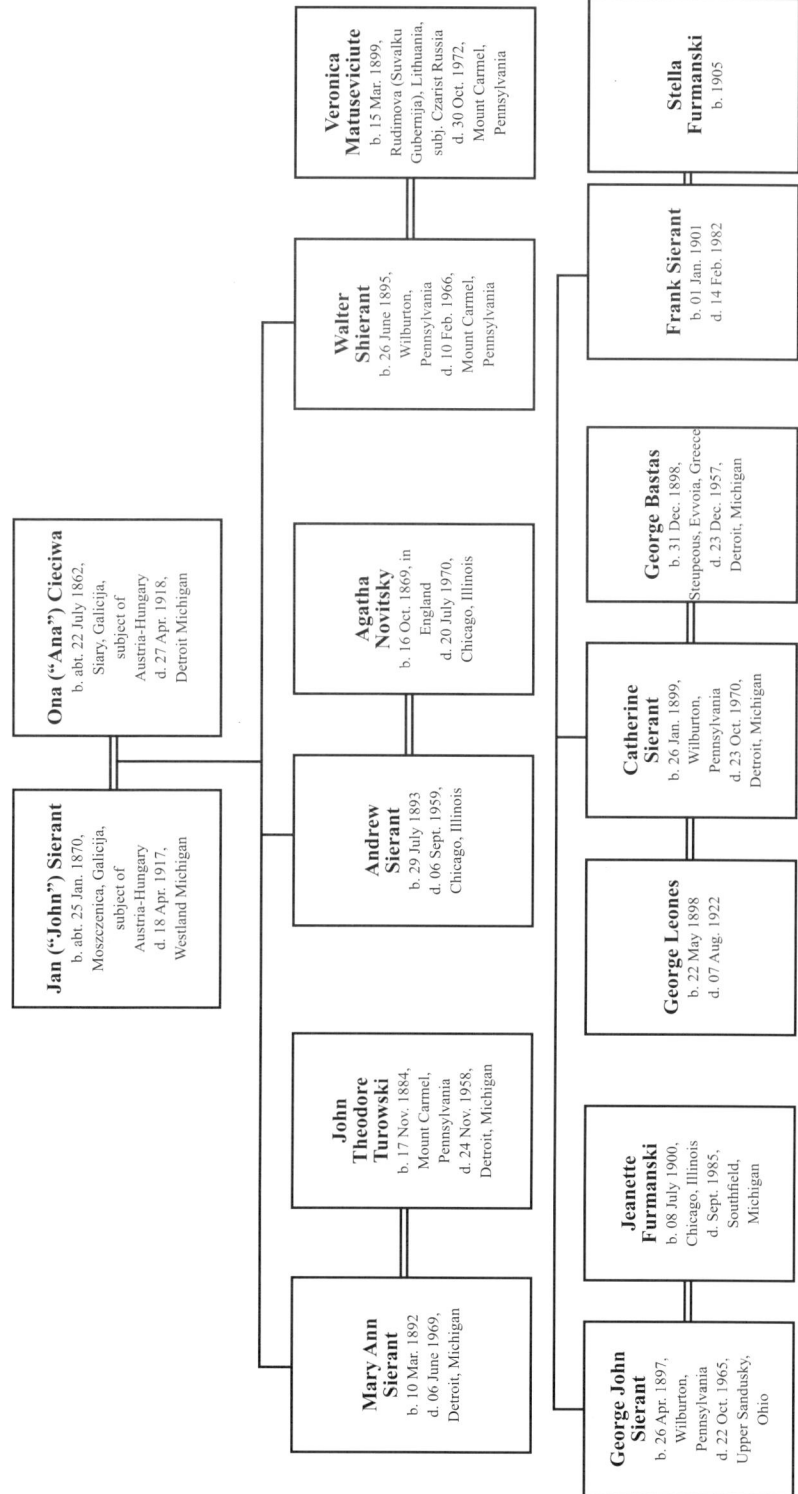

Jan ("John") Sierant
b. abt. 25 Jan. 1870,
Moszczenica, Galicija,
subject of
Austria-Hungary
d. 18 Apr. 1917,
Westland Michigan

Ona ("Ana") Cieciwa
b. abt. 22 July 1862,
Siary, Galicija,
subject of
Austria-Hungary
d. 27 Apr. 1918,
Detroit Michigan

Veronica Matuseviciute
b. 15 Mar. 1899,
Rudimova (Suvalku
Gubernija), Lithuania,
subj. Czarist Russia
d. 30 Oct. 1972,
Mount Carmel,
Pennsylvania

Stella Furmanski
b. 1905

Walter Shierant
b. 26 June 1895,
Wilburton,
Pennsylvania
d. 10 Feb. 1966,
Mount Carmel,
Pennsylvania

Frank Sierant
b. 01 Jan. 1901
d. 14 Feb. 1982

Agatha Novitsky
b. 16 Oct. 1869, in
England
d. 20 July 1970,
Chicago, Illinois

George Bastas
b. 31 Dec. 1898,
Steupeous, Evvoia, Greece
d. 23 Dec. 1957,
Detroit, Michigan

Andrew Sierant
b. 29 July 1893
d. 06 Sept. 1959,
Chicago, Illinois

Catherine Sierant
b. 26 Jan. 1899,
Wilburton,
Pennsylvania
d. 23 Sept. 1970,
Detroit, Michigan

John Theodore Turowski
b. 17 Nov. 1884,
Mount Carmel,
Pennsylvania
d. 24 Nov. 1958,
Detroit, Michigan

George Leones
b. 22 May 1898
d. 07 Aug. 1922

Mary Ann Sierant
b. 10 Mar. 1892
d. 06 June 1969,
Detroit, Michigan

Jeanette Furmanski
b. 08 July 1900,
Chicago, Illinois
d. Sept. 1985,
Southfield,
Michigan

George John Sierant
b. 26 Apr. 1897,
Wilburton,
Pennsylvania
d. 22 Oct. 1965,
Upper Sandusky,
Ohio

Historical Documents

The following items are samples of the kinds of official documents that were uncovered during the research for this book and from which many of the facts recounted were obtained—especially "vital data" such as dates and places of birth, immigration, marriage, death, etc.

Much of the challenge, and pleasure, of family history research is the "detective work" needed to locate documents such as these. Fortunately there are many excellent genealogical reference books that tell where and how to seek documentary evidence about the people and places being researched.

"ON JUNE 22, 1901, JAN REGISTERED FOR NATURALIZATION"
Jan Siewart Declaration of Intention, from files of Northumberland County, Pennsylvania

"ANA DIED APRIL 27, 1918"
Anna (Ana) Sierant Death Certificate, from State of Michigan, Division of Vital Statistics

No. 907

Form 2202
Department of Commerce and Labor
NATURALIZATION SERVICE

TRIPLICATE
(To be given to the person making the Declaration)

UNITED STATES OF AMERICA

DECLARATION OF INTENTION

(Invalid for all purposes seven years after the date hereof)

State of **Pennsylvania** } ss:
County of **Northumberland**

In the **Common Pleas** Court
of **Northumberland County**

I, **Martin Matusevicz**, aged **36** years,
occupation **Miner**, do declare on oath that my personal
description is: Color **White**, complexion **Light**, height **5** feet **2** inches,
weight **160** pounds, color of hair **Brown**, color of eyes **Brown**
other visible distinctive marks **Small pox marks on face**
I was born in **Rudamina, Russia**
on the **1st** day of **November**, anno Domini 1 **875**; I now reside
at **No. 310 South Maple Street, Mt. Carmel, Pennsylvania**
(Give number, street, city or town, and State.)
I emigrated to the United States of America from **Rotterdam, Holland**
on the vessel **Unable to obtain name after inquiry**: my last
(If the alien arrived otherwise than by vessel, the character of conveyance or name of transportation company should be given.)
foreign residence was **Rudamina, Russia**
It is my bona fide intention to renounce forever all allegiance and fidelity to any foreign
prince, potentate, state, or sovereignty, and particularly to **Nicholas II Emperor**
of all the Russias, of whom I am now a subject:
I arrived at the port of **New York**, in the
State of **New York**, on or about the **15th** day
of **August**, anno Domini 1 **901**; I am not an anarchist; I am not a
polygamist nor a believer in the practice of polygamy; and it is my intention in good faith
to become a citizen of the United States of America and to permanently reside therein:
SO HELP ME GOD. *Witness to mark*
A. C. Marulok.
Martin X Malusewicz
mark
(Original signature of declarant.)

Subscribed and sworn to before me this **8th**
day of **January**, anno Domini 191 **2**.

[SEAL]

James W. Reamer, Deputy
Clerk of the **Common Pleas** Court.

By _____ Clerk.

11—2202

"MARTINAS MATUSEVICIUS . . . WAS BORN IN RUDAMINA . . . ."
*His Declaration of Intention to become an American citizen,
under his American name, Martin Matusevicz*

"AFTER . . . JOE'S DEATH I DISCOVERED THE NATURALIZATION CERTIFICATE . . . ."
Officially "Joseph Guzievyc," he was always
Juozas Guzevicius to family and friends

Subject Index

Name Index